The Mark of a Christian

Emlen S. Garrett

xulon PRESS

Other items –

Hymns and quotes used in this book are either Public Domain or are from my head.

It would be impossible to credit every source I've learned from. I've listened to and read so many insights over the past 6 years that it's just not possible to remember everywhere I obtained a nugget. I've tried, in all circumstances, to state in my own words that which I've learned, and not directly copy another's work.

And an inscription also was written over Him in letters of Greek, Latin, and Hebrew: THIS IS THE KING OF THE JEWS.

Luke 23:38

I've used the New King James Version (NKJV) for all verses in this book unless specifically noted at the end of the verse. The other two versions I used, the King James Version (KJV) and the Darby, are both in the Public Domain. I'd like to thank those who so diligently strived to bring us the NKJV in easy to read English. They've added past centuries of acquired knowledge to this translation, which was unavailable at the time the KJV was made. Additionally, I'm grateful for their foot-notations which shed light on many areas of conflict between varying source documents, and which provide fun and interesting insights into literal text readings. I can, without reservation, recommend the NKJV to the student of the Holy Bible.

Please note: I've not included the footnotes provided in the Bible, but I have retained all the words in *italics* because they show words not in the original tongues. These are words inserted by the translators for our clarification.

When you read the Holy Bible, please read the footnotes too. They spent all that time and effort inserting them for your edification. One last thing, I don't always include the entire verse in a quote, but I don't believe it's necessary, as some, to say **Psalm 119:18a** or **Psalm 119:18b**, etc., as these are not actually in any version. I never use a portion of a verse to make a point unless I'm sure that portion is sufficient for the purpose and will not change the intent of the entire verse.

Table of Contents

The Mark vii

Preface ix

Chapter 1 – Yes, I'm a Christian… 13

Chapter 2 – The Wonderful One 27

Chapter 3 – The Trinity 35

Chapter 4 – About Baptism 55

Chapter 5 – A Day to Honor the Lord 65

Chapter 6 – Concerning Prayer 79

Chapter 7 – Tithing or Giving 93
              The Law or Grace

Chapter 8 – Eternal Salvation 103

Chapter 9 – Grace, Grace - God's Grace 111

Chapter 10 – The Generational Curse 123

Chapter 11 – Parallels 127

Chapter 12 – Prophetic Pictures...135

Chapter 13 – What Love Is 141

Chapter 14 – Glorious Scripture!...153

Final Note – The Mark of a Christian 171

Addendum – Excerpt from <u>The Translators to the Reader</u> of
the 1611 King James Version 183

Credits 189

"Go through the midst of the city, through the midst of Jerusalem, and put a mark on the foreheads of the men who sigh and cry over all the abominations that are done within it."

Ezekiel 9:4

The Mark: Drawn by Hideko Garrett

Preface

Worthy is the Lamb who was slain To receive power and riches and wisdom, And strength and honor and glory and blessing!

Revelation 5:12

1) This book was written with the idea of helping Christians through the maze of contrasting viewpoints on what marks or identifies a person as a Christian. I've endeavored to provide useful and fun information for anyone, from a young believer to the more studious members in the congregation. May it be a blessing to you and may the Lord Jesus alone be credited for anything good or useful that you may find.

2) Some of what I've put in this book came from my website, www.wonderful1.com. However, new information has been added to what's on the site.

3) There's no way I can credit every source I've learned from. I've listened to and read so many insights over the past 6 years that it's just not possible to remember everywhere I obtained a nugget. Therefore, outside of the Credits page at the end, I'd like to thank all in the Body of Christ for participating in

some way in this book. We're all being built into a Spiritual Temple and support each other as we grow.

4) I hold to a literal and complete interpretation of the Holy Bible. If a church tradition is not supported by the Scriptures, or if in my opinion a denomination, author, preacher, evangelist, creed – or whatever – is not supported by the Bible, it's not worth contemplating. We have God's full intent and purpose for mankind wrapped up in the 66 books of the Holy Bible. We need no other input to live content, full lives in Christ.

5) If you don't read your Bible everyday, please make a commitment to do so.

To My Master and Redeemer, Jesus Christ

As your bondservant, it is my heartfelt desire to give my life entirely to you forever. In accordance with Exodus 21:5 & 6, I declare the following:

I love you as my Master. I and my wife and children have committed our lives to you and do not want to go free from your presence. May my signature below be acceptable as an awl through my ear into you, the Door of Salvation. When you brought me out of spiritual Egypt and called me as yours, it was with the love of a caring and gracious master. Since that time, you have blessed me in every way. May my every breath and step be in line with your wishes. When I stray, rebuke me gently and have mercy on my family and me. May your Holy Spirit indwell me at all times and continue to fill me with each passing moment. I look forward to eternity with you ever mindful of my position as your lowly and humble bondservant.

Emlen S. Garrett A Bondservant of Christ

Signed, Witnessed, and Notarized on 28 October 2003

CHAPTER 1

Yes, I'm a Christian....

Of making many books *there* is no end, and much study is wearisome to the flesh.
                                                    Ecclesiastes 12:12

For 36 years, if someone asked me if I was a Christian, I would have shrugged and said, "yes" but not known the foggiest reason as to why. Then at 36, I discovered not only did I not meet God's standards as outlined in the Bible, but more to the point I was destined for condemnation and destruction. I grew up going to an Episcopal church, was baptized, confirmed, etc., and yet I didn't have a clue what Jesus came to do or how it was relevant to my life.

I'd like to ask that if you're going to take the time to read this book, or even part of it, that you would devote as much time to reading your Bible. Sure you have one! It's that book over there on the shelf with the dust all over it. Once you blow it off, open it and read it. In it you'll find wonders, joy, peace, hope, and above all, Jesus Christ!

In the verse above, King Solomon rightly states that there is no end to the making of books, at a time when hardly any had been written! Today we're inundated with books, and in religious circles there are thousands...no tens of thousands, written about the Holy Bible.

Christian bookstores have aisle after aisle of books, and I've never walked into one that wasn't bristling with customers. Yet I know very few people who've read the Holy Bible through even once. Can you really give someone an intelligent answer concerning your faith if you don't even know what the instructions are? And yet, you are admonished quite clearly in Scripture to be ready anytime to defend your faith:

> **I charge *you* therefore before God and the Lord Jesus Christ, who will judge the living and the dead at His appearing and His kingdom: Preach the word! Be ready in season *and* out of season. Convince, rebuke, exhort, with all longsuffering and teaching.**
> **2 Timothy 4:1, 2**

Therefore, if you're not going to read your Bible, why should you read this or any book about Christianity? Like any heretic, I could make up anything and tell you it's so and you have no reason not to believe me.

> **For the time will come when they will not endure sound doctrine, but according to their own desires, *because* they have itching ears, they will heap up for themselves teachers; and they will turn *their* ears away from the truth, and be turned aside to fables.**
> **2 Timothy 4:3, 4**

In this book, I will often quote Scripture, but that is not a sign of correct doctrine. By twisting Scripture, many have developed erroneous doctrine, intentionally or unintentionally, it is still sin. Just because someone quotes the Bible does not mean they have done so properly. An old and truthful saying is, "A verse taken out of context is a pretext." This is a certainty.

So ask yourself, "Where is the source of my faith?" It better not be in a book about a book or, like some very close to me, you are really wasting your time.

I once attended a church that had five ordained ministers in the congregation. They all had sound doctrine, but quite frankly some of them didn't know their Bible very well. One of them confessed that, although he read his Bible daily, he'd only read through it entirely once in his life, and he'd been a minister for 30 years! Sticking to the Psalms and the Gospels is to ignore a large portion of the Word of God, but many do just that.

If you haven't read your Bible, or if you don't read it daily, I'd like to challenge you to give it a real, concerted effort. Your lack of Biblical knowledge opens you up to deceit, cults, and at a minimum a strong rebuke from your Creator. I'll bet you have either cable or satellite TV and a VCR or DVD player. The chances are also that you make good use of them. Are you connected to the Internet? Think about how much time you spend either in front of the TV or computer and then - really, truthfully - compare it to how much time you spend reading the Bible. Consider tithing. What do you really know about the issue? I think you'd be extremely surprised to see what the Bible really says about it, and I'm confident it's been misrepresented in your own church. Later, I've devoted an entire section to this single issue. You need to build on the Rock and His Word. Anything else will lead you down the wrong path:

> **There is a way *that seems* right to a man, But its end *is* the way of death.**
>
> **Proverbs 14:12**

Think of it this way - do you believe there's a God? Do you believe he's competent to clearly explain His intentions to you? If he can create a bumble bee in all it's splendor, you must know that He can bring you His Word safely from the original writers without error. If you find this hard to accept, then you have a very small God and you are truly wasting your faith. Stop now, go get drunk and chase the wild life, because if you can't be certain of His Word, then His intention for you is unknown and there is therefore no accountability on your part.

I, however, am convinced of the Bible's accuracy and inerrancy - and there is no doubt that we are accountable to our Creator.

The Bible contains the mind of God, the state of man, the way of salvation, the doom of sinners, and the happiness of believers. Its doctrines are holy, its precepts are binding, its histories are true, and its decisions are immutable. Read it to be wise, believe it to be safe, and practice it to be holy. It contains light to direct you, food to support you, and comfort to cheer you. It is the traveler's map, the pilgrim's staff, the pilot's compass, the soldier's sword, and the Christian's charter. Here Paradise is restored, Heaven opened, and the gates of hell disclosed. *Christ* is its grand subject, our good the design, and the glory of God its end. It should fill the memory, rule the heart, and guide the feet. Read it slowly, frequently, and prayer-fully. It is a mine of wealth, a paradise of glory, and a river of pleasure. It is given you in life, will be opened at the judgement, and be remembered forever. It involves the highest responsibility, will reward the greatest labor, and will condemn all who trifle with its sacred contents.

Preface to the Gideon's Bible
– Author Unknown

God's love letter to you

The Holy Bible is unique in the entire world. Despite the common excuse, "it's full of contradictions." I can assure you there are none. There are parts of this great Book that are difficult to understand and I clearly don't understand them all, but never does the Bible contradict itself. In fact, it proves itself both internally and externally.

Which version should I read? I'm not going to bang this one over your head as some will, but until not too long ago I read the New International Version (NIV.) When I first met the Lord Jesus, my mother gave me this easy to read and well laid-out Bible and I read it probably 20 or more times before I switched. I also read every document available on versions, original texts, Biblical progression, etc. I self-studied Hebrew and Greek and can read them, but without much comprehension. I thought this would help me with making up my mind, but it didn't really. Not until I read the <u>Bible Wheel</u> by

Richard McDonough, did I make a real decision to change versions. Without getting too involved in the reason, Mr. McDonough's studies clearly showed me something that I had desperately wanted to resolve in my own mind. This specifically concerned passages such as the Johanine Comma, **1 John 5:7**, which has been dropped by most modern versions. Almost all modern scholars, conservative as well as liberal, have dismissed this as spurious. However, the Bible is unique in several ways:

It is a book of prophetic pictures.
It is a book of patterns.
It is a book of parallels.
It is a book of prophecy.

Each one of these categories proves the Bible, absolutely and indisputably. But, the internal nature of the Bible, specifically the *patterns,* proves the textual accuracy of disputed areas, such as the Johanine Comma. I could go on discussing such patterns, but suffice it to say that because of these studies, I've switched to the New King James Version, which is based on the same texts as the King James Version and the Geneva Bible. The Geneva Bible was the version used by the earliest immigrants to America. These early pilgrims and America's founding years, full of hardships and troubles, found rest in this translation. Then, the Gospel has been delivered to more generations and people through the King James Version than any other. More recently, the New King James Version was published to modernize the archaic English of the King James Version.

Do I still have questions? Yes, a thousand times over. The Dead Sea scrolls were clearly preserved by God as a witness to the reestablished Israel. They were kept hidden until just the right moment in time, 1947. One year later, Israel was reborn, exactly as predicted by the Holy Bible - to the very day! But the Dead Sea scrolls differ in some ways from the Hebrew text on which the abovementioned Bibles are based. The differences are small, but there are some. For now, I simply trust that God knows our hearts and He will resolve all these questions in the future.

One comfort for those looking for the perfect translation is the preface to the original King James Version. It's very lengthy and is no longer normally published except in a much abbreviated form. However, they address this very issue – about the use of variations in translations. Because this is such a relevant issue to many, I've included a short addendum at the end of this book with their thoughts. If this is an issue with which you are uncertain, take 10 minutes and read that addendum now.

One thing I do know concerning Bible versions is this - you aren't any more or any less saved by a version of the Bible. Your salvation, your soul's eternal destiny, is secured by an act of faith alone and everything after that moment falls into another category, rewards and loss of rewards.

> **For by grace you have been saved through faith, and that not of yourselves; *it is* the gift of God, not of works, lest anyone should boast.**
>
> **Ephesians 2:8, 9**

I mentioned the Biblical prediction of the re-establishment of Israel a moment ago. I'd like to go back to that thought for a moment. As I said, *prophecy* confirms the Bible also. When God speaks in the Bible and states something will happen, all we need do is believe and wait for it to transpire. I am surer of the rapture (because the Bible predicts it) than I am that my wife will cook me a good dinner tonight. And after 22 years of never cooking a bad one, I have no reason to think I'll be excusing her from the house tonight (tee hee.)

Another area of the Bible's uniqueness is *parallels*. The Bible has about 40 authors and was written over about 1600 years and yet there are parallels in this Book of books that fit seamlessly and could not have been pre-planned. I've devoted a short chapter to some fun parallels hidden in Scripture.

Prophetic pictures are of great interest to me. An example of such a picture is the layout of the tribes of Israel as they camped around the Tabernacle in the wilderness. Because of the beauty of this picture, I've included a short description of it in this book.

Prophecy, prophetic pictures, patterns, and parallels - the Word of God, the Holy Bible is unique and unparalleled.

People - think! How dull are your senses if you should doubt the God who would send His Son to hang on a cross for you. If He has done that, then His Word must be sure. I'd like to challenge you to start reading your Bible 30 minutes a day. When you read it, ask yourself, "How does this point to Christ Jesus?" Old or New Testament, the Bible tells us of God's relationship with man and the redemption of mankind through Jesus Christ.

The heart of the matter - What do I believe?

As a preface to this subsection, I'd like to acknowledge that if you're going to quit reading this book early, it will probably happen here. There's no point in giving the Good News or instruction until the truth of the matter concerning our relationship with the Creator is addressed. Far too often, preachers focus their ministries only on the love of God, His willingness to bless us, His mercy, and His compassion. These are all important aspects of our relationship with Him and make great sermons, but without introducing sin, sin's consequences, judgment, condemnation, etc., they aren't completing the picture of this relationship.

It seems like once a month you hear the results of a study concerning religion, whether it's about America, Europe, Asia, or a comparison between any of the above. I heard one recently that said 70 million Americans claimed to be Bible-believing Christians. This simply isn't true, because if it were there wouldn't be homosexuals in public office, there wouldn't be abortion on demand, and the public display of the Ten Commandments wouldn't be an issue. If these 70 million people believed the Bible, they would vote according to Biblical precepts and these problems wouldn't be in the public spectrum. If you claim to be a Christian, what do you believe concerning the following?

(1) There is more than one way to God or that Christianity provides the only way to salvation.
(2) You are an inherently good person.
(3) God will overlook the bad you've done because of the good you've done to make up for it.

Your answers to these and similar questions will indicate your understanding of what it means to be a Christian. As I said before, until a few years ago had you asked me if I were a Christian, I would have said "sure" without knowing the foggiest reason why, other than that I'd attended an Episcopal church growing up. Unfortunately, that wouldn't have been an acceptable answer to the Judge of all mankind when my days had ended.

Jesus was very clear about the path to God:

Jesus said to him, "I am the way, the truth, and the life. No one comes to the Father except through Me."

John 14:6

When the Lord said this, He wasn't saying He was one of many ways. It's crystal clear that He was indicating a very narrow road to ultimate salvation, and He is it.

About being inherently good - that's a great lie from the devil! King David, Israel's sweet Psalmist understood the inherent corruption of man:

Behold, I was brought forth in iniquity, And in sin my mother conceived me.

Psalm 51:5

Paul discusses this in the Book of **Ephesians**:

And you *He made alive,* who were dead in trespasses and sins, in which you once walked according to the course of this world, according to the prince of the power of the air, the spirit who now works in the sons of disobedience, among whom also we all once conducted ourselves in the

lusts of our flesh, fulfilling the desires of the flesh and of the mind, and were by nature children of wrath, just as the others.

Ephesians 2:1-3

Concerning works to please God:

But we are all like an unclean *thing,* And all our righteousnesses *are* like filthy rags; We all fade as a leaf, And our iniquities, like the wind, Have taken us away.

Isaiah 64:6

No works that you do will be pleasing to God, ever, without first dealing with the sin problem in your life. According to the Bible, there's a rift or fracture between God and man that we cannot overcome. There is no good work that we can do to please God until we are first in a right standing with Him. Then, if we can't do a good work to please Him, how can we bring ourselves into a right standing? This is a real dilemma, and outside of Christ Jesus no other religious expression even addresses the issue. In other words, just as Jesus said that He is the Way the Truth and the Life, he makes it clear that no other form of religion is acceptable to God because our works cannot please Him. It is Christ who prepares the way and without Christ the expression is initiated by us and is work-based. Only Christianity provides for salvation outside of works. Even the law, which sustained the people of Israel, only pointed to the coming Redeemer:

Therefore the law was our tutor *to bring us* to Christ, that we might be justified by faith. But after faith has come, we are no longer under a tutor.

Galatians 3:24, 25

As cold as this is going to sound, all the death, pain, suffering, religious fanaticism, etc., in the world ultimately doesn't matter to the individual soul. When 250,000 people including children, women, and the aged were wiped out in Indonesia during the great tsunami, it made no difference to the disposition of their eternal souls. The reason why is because those who were Christians will be raised again by the power of God through Christ Jesus to eternal life. His resurrection proved this and His Word confirms it will occur. Those who were not Christians stood *condemned already* according to Scripture. These souls will face what is termed The Great White Throne judgment in the book of **Revelation**. Their fate was sealed through the sin of Adam:

> **He who believes in Him is not condemned; but he who does not believe is condemned already, because he has not believed in the name of the only begotten Son of God.**
>
> **John 3:18**

This is the reason why true, blood-bought Christians serve so diligently as missionaries or so generously support their missionaries; why Christians evangelize the lost; why they pray so fervently for loved ones. The truth is that without Christ, all souls are *condemned already*.

Yes, in my human mind I find this almost impossible, but through the words of the Bible it is confirmed. If you are throwing your hands up right now in anger, it doesn't change your standing with God. Bitterness at a concept or teaching of God doesn't change its truth:

> **But indeed, O man, who are you to reply against God? Will the thing formed say to him who formed *it*, "Why have you made me like this?" Does not the potter have power over the clay, from the same lump to make one vessel for honor and another for dishonor?**
>
> **Romans 9:20, 21**

I once heard a really liberal Presbyterian preacher quote the verse that states:

> **For it pleased *the Father that* in Him all the fullness should dwell, and by Him to reconcile all things to Himself, by**

Him, whether things on earth or things in heaven, having made peace through the blood of His cross.

Colossians 1:19, 20

His teaching at this Bible study was rather shallow. He said "the word 'all' in the Greek means 'all.'" His logic was that even the bad and those who have not trusted Jesus would still be reconciled. So much for free will! Anyway, two points on this logic:

(1) He failed to read the verse just down the page, which says that giant word "if." If is a conditional word and clearly those outside the "if" are not included in the positive sense.

(2) Yes, all things are reconciled through the cross - some to salvation and eternal rest and some to condemnation. If you've been instructed in such a manner and believe it, you need to spend more time comparing Scripture to Scripture and less listening to liberal doctrine.

The Bible never teaches "universal salvation." Nor, going to the other extreme, does it teach salvation by works. Despite such falsi-ties, to be saved there is no requirement to speak in tongues, have a particular denominational affiliation, or any other such nonsense. From first to last, salvation is of the Lord by grace, through faith. We are given insights into what fruits should be evident in a saved believer, but these come *from* the gift of salvation, not the other way around.

So ask yourself, "What do I believe?" Is it ok to pray to Mary or the saints? Do I need to give ten percent (a tithe) to church? Is baptism required? Do I have to observe the Sabbath on Saturday, or Sunday worship? If I am saved, can I lose my salvation? Is the doctrine of the Trinity correct or are those guys with white shirts and black ties that keep coming to my front door right? If you can't answer these questions from the Bible, how can you know if it's true or just the teaching of man? I'll address all of these questions and more and give verses and or logic to support each, but unless you read and learn the Bible, you're again relying on someone other than

God to show you the truth of the matter. The following is what I do before reading Scripture and may be a help to you as you conduct a Bible reading program:

Each day, before you begin your Bible study, go to **Psalm 119**. This is the longest chapter in the Bible, containing 176 verses. However, it is broken down into 22 octaves. Each verse in an octave begins with a letter from the Hebrew aleph-bet. The first letter is Aleph and verses 1-8 in the Hebrew begin with Aleph, the second letter is Beth and verses 9-16 begin with Beth, etc. This is known as an acrostic.

There are several acrostics in the Bible and are a valuable memorization tool and also a means of expression. As an example, the book of **Lamentations is based on acrostics, but as the book progresses, there are divergences from the normal 22-letter pattern and finally a total breakdown of the acrostic. In this case it was a symbol of the total breakdown of the society during the siege and overthrow of Jerusalem.**

One wonderful aspect of **Psalm 119** is that almost every verse mentions God's Word in one term or another (judgments, testimonies, word, precept, law, etc.) and asks God to open His Word to you.

> **Open my eyes, that I may see Wondrous things from Your law.**
>
> **Psalm 119:18**

If you use **Psalm 119** as your daily introduction to Scripture reading and as a prayer of petition, do you honestly think God will reject this cry? At the end of 22 days, you will have read the entire Psalm at which time you can start again. This has been my daily practice since I first realized what a valuable tool it is. Read these two verses from **Psalm 119** and rejoice:

> **99a I have more understanding than all my teachers.**
> **102b For You Yourself have taught me.**

As you grow in your knowledge of the Word, you too will find the same joy as the Psalmist of old:

How sweet are Your words to my taste, *Sweeter* **than honey to my mouth!**

Psalm 119:103

I ask you now, commit to reading the Bible everyday. Pray for enlightenment as you do and seek God's face in the wonderful words He has given us.

What is the mark of a Christian? You claim the title, but you may not be sure why. Together, let's go over some of the fundamental truths that identify a person as a follower of the Lord Jesus. Turn the page and let's discover Christ Jesus and a little about the Christian Church.

CHAPTER 2

The Wonderful One

All authority has been given to Me in heaven and on earth.

Matthew 28:18

The Bible, among other things, explains God's relationship with man and the redemption of man through Christ Jesus. If you study ancient Hebrew script you'll see that the Wonderful Cross is hidden in the very middle of the first sentence of the Bible. From the first sentence to the last, Jesus Christ is the focus. He is the object of the Christian faith, He is the only source of a Christian's hope, He is our Salvation, our Rock, our Redeemer, our Hiding Place and our Safe Refuge. He is the Wonderful One full of grace and truth, and from Him alone springs all hope, joy, peace, patience, and longsuffering. He is the Mighty God, the Balm of Gilead, and the Rose of Sharon. In all ways, Jesus Christ is the sole purpose and point of our existence and without that focus life has no meaning.

Volumes have been written about Jesus, and into eternity more can and will be written. Forever, the saints will sing of His love and goodness. For this reason, you might think this would be the longest chapter of the book, but I've decided to keep it very brief and also to merely give a short discussion of why we so desperately need this God/Man link.

First though, a portion of Paul's discourse on Christ's preeminence from **Colossians:**

> **He is the image of the invisible God, the firstborn over all creation. For by Him all things were created that are in heaven and that are on earth, visible and invisible, whether thrones or dominions or principalities or powers. All things were created through Him and for Him. And He is before all things, and in Him all things consist. And He is the head of the body, the church, who is the beginning, the firstborn from the dead, that in all things He may have the preeminence. For it pleased *the Father that* in Him all the fullness should dwell, and by Him to reconcile all things to Himself, by Him, whether things on earth or things in heaven, having made peace through the blood of His cross.**
>
> **Colossians 1:15-20**

I can (and have) read this description over and over again, and yet I can't grasp the weight of what he describes. A man died on a wooden cross, naked and alone, 2000 years ago and yet He has directed the entire course of human history and beyond. He holds the universe together by His own power, and He established a Church, a living Temple, through His death and resurrection. He has brought peace *through* His shed blood. I simply can't comprehend the enormity of Jesus Christ and yet here I am trying to in my limited, imperfect self. What an honor to pursue the knowledge of this Great and Awesome God! What a joy to pass on to others the little I have learned!

Why the Cross?

What is it that brought us to the point where we need a Savior? Just what is Jesus saving us from?

The Bible teaches that man was created. Yes, yes, I know - you've been taught that we evolved from a lightning bolt energizing a bowl of lentil soup and amino acids. Eventually, this stuff made it up to a fish and then a platypus, then a monkey and somehow, accidentally the monkey fell from a tree and split one of its zygotes, which ruptured its DNA and nine months later out popped a little baby human.

The fact is that there is not one, not a single, piece of evidence for evolution. It is a lie. Another of the devil's greatest. Through the teaching of evolution, we can exterminate millions of "lesser humans," and for the sake of convenience we can kill unborn babies, both without any moral dilemma at all. Because of this teaching, there is no moral absolute - no Creator, no original sin, no account-ability. Yes, we were created, and yes, we are accountable.

The first chapter of **Romans** so clearly tells us about the condi-tion of those who deny this fundamental truth:

> **For the wrath of God is revealed from heaven against all ungodliness and unrighteousness of men, who suppress the truth in unrighteousness, because what may be known of God is manifest in them, for God has shown *it* to them. For since the creation of the world His invisible *attributes* are clearly seen, being understood by the things that are made, *even* His eternal power and Godhead, so that they are without excuse, because, although they knew God, they did not glorify *Him* as God, nor were thankful, but became futile in their thoughts, and their foolish hearts were darkened. Professing to be wise, they became fools, and changed the glory of the incorruptible God into an image made like corruptible man—and birds and four-footed animals and creeping things.**
>
> **Romans 1:18-23**

When God created man, He did it in such a loving and contem-plative way that we can discern thousands of different smells and tastes. We have the ability to weigh the entire universe while sitting on an infinitesimally small planet on an outer band of a galaxy in a universe of millions of galaxies. We can reason, love, adore, feel, sense. In His glorious mercy He gave us free will. If we don't want to acknowledge Him, we don't have to. We can shake our puny little fists in His face and act as if we run the show when we can't even handle our close relationships properly. But what good is a creature that can't reciprocate its love and affection? God could have whipped us together in such a way that we would sing "Holy, Holy, Holy" all day and night like a robot, but this would mean nothing. Freewill however allows a two-way relationship. And so, in this way we were formed. When God made man, he did so knowing that man would sin...I have no doubt of this, He is the Beginning and the End. But sin we did, and this when there was only one command, and that in the negative, *you shall not.* Because of this sin of disobedience, a fracture occurred - a separation between the eternally holy, righteous, and judicious God and His rebellious creature. The devil tempted man and man accepted the devil's leadership. You don't believe me? Proof is in the encounter of Jesus with the devil at the beginning of His earthly ministry:

> **Then the devil, taking Him up on a high mountain, showed Him all the kingdoms of the world in a moment of time. And the devil said to Him, "All this authority I will give You, and their glory; for *this* has been delivered to me, and I give it to whomever I wish."**
>
> **Luke 4:5, 6**

Man, the first man, chose the devil's lie over God. We, from that moment fell under the curse of death and the control of Satan because we are under the federal headship of Adam. When God condemned Adam, all of Adam's progeny stood condemned *through him.* Whether you voted for George Bush or not, you must submit to his federal authority. When he signs a law, you are obligated to obey it. When Adam sinned, we took on his sin nature. Proof of this concept is found in **Romans 5** where Christ's work is shown to override the evil deed of our first father, Adam:

> **Therefore, as through one man's offense *judgment came* to all men, resulting in condemnation, even so through one Man's righteous act *the free gift came* to all men, resulting in justification of life. For as by one man's disobedience**

**many were made sinners, so also by one Man's obedience
many will be made righteous.**

Romans 5:18, 19

This verse helps explain Jesus' words to Nicodemus in **John
3:5, 6**:

**Jesus answered, "Most assuredly, I say to you, unless
one is born of water and the Spirit, he cannot enter the
kingdom of God. That which is born of the flesh is flesh,
and that which is born of the Spirit is spirit.**

It is through acceptance of Christ that we move from the federal
headship of Adam - that of death and condemnation, to that of Jesus
- being born again of the Spirit:

**And so it is written, *"The first man Adam became a
living being."* The last Adam *became* a life-giving spirit.
However, the spiritual is not first, but the natural, and
afterward the spiritual. The first man *was* of the earth,
made of dust; the second Man *is* the Lord from heaven.
As *was* the *man* of dust, so also *are* those *who are made* of
dust; and as *is* the heavenly *Man,* so also *are* those *who are*
heavenly. And as we have borne the image of the *man* of
dust, we shall also bear the image of the heavenly *Man.***

1 Corinthians 15:45-49

It was through Christ's perfect obedience to the Father that He
prevailed. However, that still hasn't taken care of *our* problem – that
we owe a debt, payable because of the sins we have committed. It
was for this reason that Jesus went to the cross. Let's take a real life
example to help you understand:

*I speed down the highway at 127 mph. The speed limit is 70
mph. I get caught and, not only do I have to pay a fine, I was
going so fast that I have to go see the judge – probably so he
can ask me about the high performance engine I installed.*

Maybe he's curious where he can get one... well, probably not. Anyway, I go to the judge, he tells me what's on his mind and then says I owe $550. Unfortunately, I spent all my money on that engine work.... He says, "Pay the fine or go to jail." I'm a goner, for sure. However, at just that moment, my lawyer pulls out his wallet and says, "I'll pay the bill. Plus, there's no legal fee!" The judge accepts the money on behalf of the state. The fine is paid and I am set free.

It's unimaginable that an earthly lawyer would do this for any of us, and yet this is similar, although a somewhat simplistic example, of what Jesus did. I've heard it said:

We owed a debt we could not pay; He paid a debt He did not owe.

Not only did Jesus live the perfect life, but He also paid our sin-debt at the cross. When we put our trust in Him, we move from death to life and our transgressions are cast away, never to be remembered again.

I'll re-explain this again as a reminder and provide further clarification as we go on. But for now, suffice it to say that the Creator of the Universe, God Almighty, accomplished this action. I say this, knowing there are many who claim Jesus is not God. However, most of the New Testament epistles' strongest warnings deal with precisely the issue of the Lord's divinity. I don't believe there's anything so clear – so crystal clear – as the divinity of our Lord and the nature of the Godhead. And yet people are so easily led astray by false teachers and ravenous wolves. The next chapter is devoted specifically to the Trinity and it's my heartfelt desire that you not only contemplate it, but also research the matter yourself.

As many believers throughout the years have actually grown in theological knowledge from music, I'd like you to consider the words of Charles H. Gabriel in the hymn My Savior's Love:

I stand amazed in the presence Of Jesus the Nazarene, And wonder how He could love me, A sinner, condemned, unclean.

For me it was in the garden He prayed: "Not My will, but Thine." He had no tears for His own griefs, But sweat drops of blood for mine.

In pity angels beheld Him, And came from the world of light To comfort Him in the sorrows He bore for my soul that night.

He took my sins and my sorrows, He made them His very own; He bore the burden to Calvary, And suffered and died alone.

When with the ransomed in glory His face I at last shall see, 'Twill be my joy through the ages To sing of His love for me.

O how marvelous! O how wonderful! And my song shall ever be: O how marvelous! O how wonderful! Is my Savior's love for me!

It is the mark of a Christian to understand that we owe a sin-debt and that we cannot pay it on our own. Instead, Christians understand that Jesus Christ came in the flesh to live the perfect life and then give His life as a ransom for us. By faith, a Christian reaches out to Jesus, acknowledges he is a sinner and that he cannot save himself.

CHAPTER 3

The Trinity

"Holy, holy, holy is the LORD of hosts; The whole earth is full of His glory!"

Isaiah 6:3

One of the most important tenants of true Christianity is the concept of the Trinity. The Trinity is clearly presented throughout the Holy Bible and its denial is a sure sign of apostasy. However, it was one of the mysteries long hidden at God's prerogative. I wonder how the ancient Hebrews felt as they worshipped the one true God without fully recognizing this part of His eternal character. It was not until Christ that the mystery of this profound secret was finally revealed:

> Now to Him who is able to establish you according to my gospel and the preaching of Jesus Christ, according to the revelation of the mystery kept secret since the world began but now made manifest, and by the prophetic Scriptures made known to all nations, according to the commandment of the everlasting God, for obedience to the faith—to God, alone wise, *be* glory through Jesus Christ forever. Amen.
>
> **Romans 16:25-27**

The doctrine of the Trinity states that God has a threefold nature or character and yet they together are one God. This Trinity as revealed through Holy Scripture is:

The Father
The Son
The Holy Spirit

In the Holy Bible, at one time or another, the term "He" is used to describe each separate part of this eternal Godhead and helps solidify our faith in this concept. When Jesus uttered the Great Commission to his apostles, He said the following:

Go therefore and make disciples of all the nations, baptizing them in the name of the Father and of the Son and of the Holy Spirit, teaching them to observe all things that I have commanded you; and lo, I am with you always, *even* to the end of the age." Amen.
Matthew 28:19, 20

Here Jesus cites that baptism is to be conducted in the name (singular) of the Father and of the Son and of the Holy Spirit. In the original Greek, the word "name" (onoma) is singular as well - each of these entities combines into one essence. Can we find a parallel in the Old Testament?

Deuteronomy 6:4 is known to the Jewish people as the Sh'ma (Hear), the Hebrew statement of faith from ages past which has been repeated thousands of times a day everyday since it was first uttered by Moses in the desert at the base of Mount Sinai:

Sh'ma Yisrael YHVH Elohaynu YHVH Echad
Hear, O Israel: the LORD our God, the LORD is One!

In this Sh'ma, it says, **"The LORD is One."** A cluster of grapes is one; the people Israel are one people. Both of these examples are made up of individual parts and yet are termed "one." The word "echad" enables this interpretation. There is another Hebrew word which means one and only one that could have been used, yachid. However, it was not used. The use of yachid is not without Biblical precedent:

Then He said, "Take now your son, your only *son* Isaac, whom you love, and go to the land of Moriah, and offer him there as a burnt offering on one of the mountains of which I shall tell you."

Genesis 22:2

"Only" in this case is the word yachid.

We can rightly assume that the Creator knows Hebrew even better than any of us do! However, the term "echad" was used in **Deuteronomy 6:4**. Another such Old Testament reference is the word for God in Hebrew that is used over 3000 times, even from the first sentence of the Bible. The word is "Elohim." Elohim by its very nature in Hebrew indicates a possible plurality or fullness. When the Hebrew language moves a word from the singular to plural "im" is often added. This is comparable to "s" in English. For example, a type of angel is a cherub; the plural is cherubim. A different angel found in **Isaiah** is a seraph, but two or more would be seraphim. And so forth.

Throughout the ages since the church was established, people have used tangible concepts to try to explain this Trinity, such as water as steam, liquid, or solid. Or, a circle divided into three equal parts, etc. However, neither of these accurately portrays the concept, and in fact if used can lead to heresy. Is it that there is no corresponding parallel? Has God left us with a concept but no way to properly explain it? The really interesting fact is that a concept has been provided, and it is visible everywhere you look. If you have time for some very interesting reading, you should obtain the book The Secret of the Universe, by Dr. Nathan R. Wood. Dr. Wood, who once was president of Gordon College of Theology and Missions, states that the Trinity is revealed in the universe itself.

A brief explanation of this is that the universe is comprised of a trinity of Space, Time, and Matter. Furthermore, each of these is a trinity itself. Space is comprised of Length, Breadth, and Height. Time is expressed in Past, Present, and Future. And matter consists of Energy in Motion producing Phenomena. How wonderful...a trinity of trinities!

Continuing on this same line, it's possible to equate Space with the Father - unseen and yet omnipresent; Matter with the Son - visible, tangible, audible, understandable; and Time with the Spirit - which is unseen and yet it is a medium in which we move and obtain understanding.

Again, Dr. Wood takes the concept of Time, and with true inspiration breaks it down into an understandable concept. After doing this, he changes only four words and thereby explains the mystery of the Trinity in a manner we can comprehend. In my own words, I'll try to explain his most excellent dissertation on the subject. However, I recommend his book for the serious student of the Bible. Here I will follow his same pattern of substitution. In short this concept says:

Time is comprised of Future, Present, and Past. The Future is an unknowable and unseen entity – always out of reach except as presented in the Present. In other words, it is the Present which continually reveals Time the Future. The Future comes first only in our reason, but not in Time because there has always been a Present as well as a Future. The difference is that we perceive and react with only the Present in Time.

The Past (to our reason) comes after the Present, again unseen, but is the point on which we can reflect on and understand the Present in Time. The Past is our instructor and our Comforter, continually replacing what we experienced in the Present. Again, as with the relationship of the Future to the Present, the Present comes first only in our reason, but not in Time because there has always been a Past as well as a Present. The Past merely issues from the Present.

In essence, there is a continuous stream of Time going from the Future to the Present to the Past. Each has always existed and always will exist and each has a purpose in the life of man, but only the Present is tangible, visible, audible - what is comprehendible to our human senses. It is the Present that makes the Future understandable and it is the Past which reminds us of our Time as the Present. We can only look forward to the Future in anticipation, and the Past helps us live in the Present because of the illumination provided.

The next step is to simply change Future, Present, Past and Time to read Father, Son, Holy Spirit, and God.

God is comprised of Father, Son, and Holy Spirit. The Father is an unknowable and unseen entity – always out of reach except as presented in the Son. In other words, it is the Son which continually reveals God the Father. The Father comes first only in our reason, but not in God because there has always been a Son as well as a Father. The difference is that we perceive and react with only the Son in God.

The Holy Spirit (to our reason) comes after the Son, again unseen, but is the point on which we can reflect on and understand the Son in God. The Holy Spirit is our instructor and our Comforter, continually replacing what we experienced in the Son. Again, as with the relationship of the Father to the Son, the Son comes first only in our reason, but not in God because there has always been a Holy Spirit as well as a Son. The Holy Spirit merely issues from the Son.

In essence, there is a continuous stream of God going from the Father to the Son to the Holy Spirit. Each has always existed and always will exist and each has a purpose in the life of man, but only the Son is tangible, visible, audible - what is comprehendible to our human senses. It is the Son that makes the Father understandable and it is the Holy Spirit which reminds us of our God as the Son. We can only look forward to the Father in anticipation, and the Holy Spirit helps us live in the Son because of the illumination provided.

And there we have what has been evident since creation in the physical universe as demonstrated in Time and to which Holy Scripture so faithfully testifies in the nature of the Godhead. While contemplating this myself I must agree with Dr. Wood's analysis, because we *anticipate* God through the Father, just as we anticipate Time through the Future. We *come into contact* with God through the Son, just as we come into contact with Time through the Present. Finally, we're *left with the remembrance* of our contact with God through our relationship with the Holy Spirit, just as our remembrance of Time is based on the Past. All this is just as the Bible portrays each member of the Godhead. I find no contradiction in any Biblical description. It is true, God is much more richly described in Scripture, but the essence of the roles fits this model in an exceptional way.

Remember one thing concerning time; we tend to think of ourselves coming out of the past. However, this simply isn't the case. We're coming out of the future, meeting it face on as it arrives, moment by moment. A simple way to explain this is to remember that Bill Clinton was once our President. George Bush was future at that point. Now Bill Clinton is history and George Bush is in office. At some point, hopefully soon, Jesus will return and become the Ruler of the Nations, but that is yet in the future.

One area where someone may immediately disagree with this presentation is when the Father's voice is heard while Jesus is present. However, I don't see any conflict with this due to the description of the voice given in **John 12:29**:

> **Therefore the people who stood by and heard *it* said that it had thundered. Others said, "An angel has spoken to Him."**

The voice is not necessarily the voice of a tangible, physical presence, but is possibly the manipulation of nature in such a way as to provide expression. Throughout Scripture, God works *through* nature to make His presence known and, although we don't know the means used at this time, this may be what occurred here.

From this point, I'll give several of the hundreds of quotes directly from the Holy Bible supporting this striking viewpoint concerning the Godhead as explained above.

About the Trinity

Then God said, "Let Us make man in Our image, according to Our likeness; let them have dominion over the fish of the sea, over the birds of the air, and over the cattle, over all the earth and over every creeping thing that creeps on the earth."

Genesis 1:26

Here in the first chapter of Scripture the term "Us" is used by the Creator reflecting His triune nature. And again, in **Isaiah**:

Also I heard the voice of the Lord, saying: " Whom shall I send, And who will go for Us?" Then I said, "Here *am* I! Send me."

Isaiah 6:8

Next, the 12th chapter of the book of **Zechariah** places all three members of the Trinity together in one passage:

"And I will pour on the house of David and on the inhabitants of Jerusalem the Spirit of grace and supplication; then they will look on Me whom they pierced. Yes, they will mourn for Him as one mourns for *his* only *son,* and grieve for Him as one grieves for a firstborn.

Zechariah 12:10

The Gospel of **John** time and again reflects the relationship between the Father and the Son as well as the Spirit:

Philip said to Him, "Lord, show us the Father, and it is sufficient for us." Jesus said to him, "Have I been with

you so long, and yet you have not known Me, Philip? He who has seen Me has seen the Father; so how can you say, 'Show us the Father'?

John 14:8, 9

Nevertheless I tell you the truth. It is to your advantage that I go away; for if I do not go away, the Helper will not come to you; but if I depart, I will send Him to you. And when He has come, He will convict the world of sin, and of righteousness, and of judgment: of sin, because they do not believe in Me; of righteousness, because I go to My Father and you see Me no more; of judgment, because the ruler of this world is judged.

John 16:7-11

Paul clearly understood God's triune nature. He alludes to it here and elsewhere many times in his epistles:

The grace of the Lord Jesus Christ, and the love of God, and the communion of the Holy Spirit *be* with you all. Amen.

2 Corinthians 13:14

I urge you in the sight of God who gives life to all things, and *before* Christ Jesus who witnessed the good confession before Pontius Pilate, that you keep *this* commandment without spot, blameless until our Lord Jesus Christ's appearing, which He will manifest in His own time, *He who is* the blessed and only Potentate, the King of kings and Lord of lords, who alone has immortality, dwelling in unapproachable light, whom no man has seen or can see, to whom *be* honor and everlasting power. Amen.

1 Timothy 6:13-16

About the Father

I'll limit my Bible passages on the Father, as it is clearly understood by every human –despite frequent denials - that there is a God
who is most commonly associated with the Father:

For since the creation of the world His invisible *attributes*
are clearly seen, being understood by the things that are
made, *even* His eternal power and Godhead, so that they
are without excuse,

Romans 1:20

Not that anyone has seen the Father, except He who is
from God; He has seen the Father.

John 6:46

This statement by Jesus in itself perfectly matches the description Dr. Wood made concerning the Father.

About the Son

In the beginning was the Word, and the Word was with
God, and the Word was God. He was in the beginning
with God. All things were made through Him, and without
Him nothing was made that was made. In Him was life,
and the life was the light of men. And the light shines in
the darkness, and the darkness did not comprehend it.

John 1:1-5

That which was from the beginning, which we have heard,
which we have seen with our eyes, which we have looked
upon, and our hands have handled, concerning the Word
of life—the life was manifested, and we have seen, and
bear witness, and declare to you that eternal life which
was with the Father and was manifested to us—

1 John 1:1, 2

I am the Alpha and the Omega, *the* **Beginning and** *the* **End, the First and the Last.**

Revelation 22:13

In the next quote, Jesus astounded his audience. They were fully aware of the meaning of the term I AM. In Hebrew, YHVH, the Tetragrammaton. By quoting the following, he was telling them "I am God."

Jesus said to them, "Most assuredly, I say to you, before Abraham was, I AM."

John 8:58

Again, the next quote leaves no doubt about the Son and His eternal relationship with the Father:

I and *My* **Father are one.**

John 10:30

Even Jesus - the Shepherd - in his accomplished mission at Calvary, his on-going intercessory mission, and his anticipated return has three parts:

Good Shepherd - **John 10:11** - Died for His flock.
Great Shepherd - **Hebrews 13:20** - Leader of His flock.
Chief Shepherd - **1 Peter 5:4** - Returning for His flock.

Luke, the author of the Gospel that bears his name and the book of **Acts**, had no doubt of Christ's divinity. Read how he carefully worded the following, which is a pattern throughout his writings (my underlining):

"Return to your own house, and tell what great things <u>God</u> has done for you." And he went his way and proclaimed throughout the whole city what great things <u>Jesus</u> had done for him.

Luke 8:39

Paul drives the point home in the following:

He is the image of the invisible God, the firstborn over all creation. For by Him all things were created that are in heaven and that are on earth, visible and invisible, whether thrones or dominions or principalities or powers. All things were created through Him and for Him. And He is before all things, and in Him all things consist. And He is the head of the body, the church, who is the beginning, the firstborn from the dead, that in all things He may have the preeminence. For it pleased *the Father that* **in Him all the fullness should dwell, and by Him to reconcile all things to Himself, by Him, whether things on earth or things in heaven, having made peace through the blood of His cross.**

Colossians 1:15-20

...whose minds the god of this age has blinded, who do not believe, lest the light of the gospel of the glory of Christ, who is the image of God, should shine on them. For we do not preach ourselves, but Christ Jesus the Lord, and ourselves your bondservants for Jesus' sake. For it is the God who commanded light to shine out of darkness, who has shone in our hearts to *give* **the light of the knowledge of the glory of God in the face of Jesus Christ.**

2 Corinthians 4:4-6

God, who at various times and in various ways spoke in time past to the fathers by the prophets, has in these last days spoken to us by *His* **Son, whom He has appointed heir of all things, through whom also He made the worlds; who being the brightness of** *His* **glory and the express image of His person, and upholding all things by the word of His power, when He had by Himself purged our sins, sat down at the right hand of the Majesty on high,**

Hebrews 1:1-3

Jesus Christ *is* the same yesterday, today, and forever.
Hebrews 13:8

About the Spirit

That which is born of the flesh is flesh, and that which is born of the Spirit is spirit. Do not marvel that I said to you, 'You must be born again.' The wind blows where it wishes, and you hear the sound of it, but cannot tell where it comes from and where it goes. So is everyone who is born of the Spirit."
John 3:6-8

For what man knows the things of a man except the spirit of the man which is in him? Even so no one knows the things of God except the Spirit of God.
1 Corinthians 2:11

Now the Lord is the Spirit; and where the Spirit of the Lord *is,* there *is* liberty.
2 Corinthians 3:17

In addition to the very obvious verses throughout Scripture which clearly point to Jesus' divinity, some of which I've quoted here, there are many, many more subtle patterns that, when taken properly, scream out to you concerning this issue. Here's one that's so easily overlooked, and yet is a wonderful example of such a confirmation. Look over the following verses and notice the same pattern in each. Then realize that the God of the Old Testament speaks the first three examples and Jesus, that same Holy God, speaks the second three. Each with a line of thought by me:

Old Testament -
Abraham, Abraham! **But the Angel of the LORD called to him from heaven and said, "Abraham, Abraham!" So he said, "Here I am." And He said, "Do not lay your hand on the lad, or do anything to him; for now I know that**

you fear God, since you have not withheld your son, your
only *son,* from Me."

Genesis 22:11, 12

Notice the emotion of this moment, so much so that words could
never begin to show us the depth of Abraham's joy and relief. It's
all the more incredible when in its New Testament parallel, God
himself did not spare His Son, His only begotten Son, for us. Here,
the man of faith is tenderly called to lay aside the knife that would
have separated him from his dearest love in the entire world. What
are you willing to sacrifice in your life in order to be a pleasing,
faithful follower of the Lord Jesus? Is there anything in all you have
that you would not forsake for His cause?

Moses, Moses! **So when the LORD saw that he turned
aside to look, God called to him from the midst of the
bush and said, "Moses, Moses!" And he said, "Here I
am." Then He said, "Do not draw near this place. Take
your sandals off your feet, for the place where you stand
is holy ground."**

Exodus 3:4, 5

God speaks to the one "faithful in all His house" from the burning
bush. This is the moment of calling for the great prophet of Israel.
Here the man "whom the Lord knew face to face" truly came face to
face with his Creator for the first time in his life. When you receive
your calling, will you be faithful in the Lord's house to meet that
calling and give of yourself unreservedly?

Samuel, Samuel! **Now the LORD came and stood and
called as at other times, "Samuel! Samuel!" And Samuel
answered, "Speak, for Your servant hears."**

1 Samuel 3:10

After being called three times previously, the young boy Samuel
is instructed by the High Priest Eli to respond to the LORD's calling.
Imagine this, the person who was to become Israel's final Judge and

who slept at the Tabernacle with the High Priest, didn't know the voice of the LORD when he first heard it. Are you being attentive to the calling of the Lord Jesus, ready to respond to His voice in your life?

<u>New Testament</u> –
Martha, Martha! **And Jesus answered and said to her, "Martha, Martha, you are worried and troubled about many things. But one thing is needed, and Mary has chosen that good part, which will not be taken away from her."**

Luke 10:41, 42

Poor Martha! Caught up in the worries and cares of the world, she never stopped to consider what is truly of value. However, she had the blessed opportunity to hear the soft words, spoken directly from the mouth of the Lord that "many things" are not always the good part. Are you so caught up in the cares and "must dos" of the world that you've failed to spend time in God's Word? This is the well from which we must drink daily to be refreshed in His goodness. And, do you spend so much time socializing and doing busy work at your church that you fail to open your heart to Christ Jesus each week for a much needed cleansing? Choose the Good Part that cannot be taken away!

Simon, Simon! **And the Lord said, "Simon, Simon! Indeed, Satan has asked for you, that he may sift *you* as wheat. But I have prayed for you, that your faith should not fail; and when you have returned to *Me*, strengthen your brethren."**

Luke 22:31, 32

The Lord Jesus, in the most tender way, tells His great Apostle and friend that the Deceiver has intentions for him, but that his Lord is on his side and will be there to strengthen him. This lesson would allow him to do the same for his brethren in the future. Have you ever considered that fiery darts, troubles, or even disasters may have been allowed in your life simply to strengthen you so that you may in turn help others?

Saul, Saul! **Then he fell to the ground, and heard a voice saying to him, "Saul, Saul, why are you persecuting Me?"**
Acts 9:4 (and recounted in Acts 22:7, and 26:14.)

Just as Moses was commissioned by God's voice out of the fire of the burning bush, Paul likewise received his commission from the voice of Jesus (God,) instructing him to go into the city and be told all the things he was destined to do. When Paul heard the Lord's call, he responded immediately. Are you willing to immediately follow the Lord's directives? Put away every obstruction that hinders you from an intimate relationship with Him.

You see, God has, in His perfect wisdom and plan, given us all we need to be fully convinced of who He is and how we can know for sure what He says is true. Even in something as simple as a double calling of a chosen instrument! Note: I have not listed all the double callings in Scripture and God did not utter all of them. However, these cited leave no doubt about the Person and Nature of Jesus Christ. I'd like to give one more example of a double calling by God, once *through* His prophetic voice in the **Psalms** and again, in fulfillment of the **Psalms** directly from the anguish of His soul:

My God, My God, why have You forsaken Me? *Why are You so* **far from helping Me,** *And from* **the words of My groaning?**
Psalm 22:1

And about the ninth hour Jesus cried out with a loud voice, saying, "Eli, Eli, lama sabachthani?" that is, *"My God, My God, why have You forsaken Me?"*
Matthew 27:46

Consider this well - the voice which spoke the heavens and the earth into existence, and the One who controls the eternal fate of all men - the Wonderful Counselor, the Mighty God, the Everlasting

Father, the Prince of Peace - crying out in the anguish of His tormented soul for the great love of His creation. At this moment, He took all of the sin, all of the guilt, all of the punishment from fallen man upon Himself. You may ask, "What is a human soul worth?" I tell you it's worth all creation and more, because the Creator paid for it with His own life. In **Psalm 8**, King David asked why God is mindful of man. I don't know the answer to this, but I know He is. How much more then should we be mindful of Him?

The Redemption of Mankind, what is it? It is the single most significant and costly act since time began. How can anyone stand guiltless who rejects so great a salvation? Come Lord Jesus, and when you do, may we stand ready for the moment.

Surely we praise our Creator - Father, Son, and Holy Spirit! Scripture, in both Testaments leaves no doubt about God's triune nature. May you be blessed as you read the Word in the future, observing and accepting the concept of the Trinity. And, as you enjoy your surroundings, think of how God carefully placed His fingerprints on the universe around you. Reflect on it and realize those fingerprints include you - unique, loved, and triune - body, soul, and spirit.

BEWARE

Because I've devoted this section to the subject of the Trinity, it would be appropriate to devote a few short lines to one of the many heretical organizations that deny this evident truth. They are the Jehovah's Witnesses. One of their principle tenants is that Christ is not God (not part of a trinity) and therefore God does not have a triune nature. To them the Holy Spirit is an active force. I am speaking from experience concerning this cult, having first been brought to the reading of Holy Scripture through them. Had it not been for Christ's intervention, these people could have deceived me. I have no animosity towards them, but rather I feel sorry for them and pray that some may be saved. They are very quickly brainwashed into believing doctrinal heresy and are misled by the precepts of the

Watchtower Society. I'm not going to spend a lot of time discussing their doctrine, but I will give one glaring example of their apostasy.

They have changed **John 1:1** to read ...and the word was "a" god. Rather than **"...and the Word was God."** They use this terminology and say Holy Scripture backs it up. It doesn't. In Greek, unless you're specifically referring to a prophet, e.g., "John is the Prophet," they will normally not use a preposition. Therefore, in Greek you would say, "I saw prophet." Translating this into English, you would then change it to, "I saw a prophet." Again, in Greek, unless specifically saying, "I rode the bicycle," you would say, "I rode bicycle." When translating it into English, you would then add "a" - such as, "I rode a bicycle." In these instances, it is understood that there is more than one prophet, or bicycle. If there were only one prophet or one bicycle in existence, you would certainly say "the prophet" or "the bicycle." If you translate "Theos en ho logos" into "the word was a god" you, by the very nature of the translation, assume there are multiple gods. This is polytheism and the greatest blaspheme. The Holy Bible, from the beginning to the end as demonstrated above, allows for one and only one God. This heresy is a centuries old one, dating back to the time of Arius, approx. 250-336 A.D.

Even if you disregard the translation of this one passage, many times in Scripture Jesus is called our Savior, our Redeemer, our Lord, and our Creator. Even the term "Immanuel" means "God with us." Jesus receives worship, He "reads the heart and mind," he forgives sins, He is all powerful, and Scripture assigns Him "glory." In the Old Testament, all of these attributes are ascribed solely to God. It can not be mistaken that Jesus is the complete revelation of Jehovah of the Old Testament, and yet the Jehovah's Witnesses still relegate Him to a created being in their doctrine. This is blasphemy which must be confessed and turned from or they will be condemned at the judgment for failing to ascribe Him the honor which He is due.

You must be very careful and yet thoughtful when you encounter these people. They are well trained and truly believe what they have been taught. Paul warned not to get into arguments or lengthy discussions with people like this. John went so far as to say the following about those who follow heretical ideas:

If anyone comes to you and does not bring this doctrine, do not receive him into your house nor greet him; for he who greets him shares in his evil deeds.

2 John -10, 11

When approached by the Jehovah's Witnesses, Mormons, or other fringe cults, give them the Gospel, give them the truth, and pray for them. That is your duty as a Christian. However, follow the Biblical admonition to not entertain them as guests.

I've read many documents which confirm this analysis on the Greek. All those in the mainstream unanimously concur that there is no subordination of the Son to the Father. Each has His own function within the Godhead and yet is equally worthy of glory, honor, and adoration. Reginald Heber understood:

Holy, holy, holy! Lord God Almighty! Early in the morning our song shall rise to Thee; Holy, holy, holy, merciful and mighty! God in three Persons, blessed Trinity!

Holy, holy, holy! All the saints adore Thee, Casting down their golden crowns around the glassy sea; Cherubim and seraphim falling down before Thee, Who was, and is, and evermore shall be.

Holy, holy, holy! though the darkness hide Thee, Though the eye of sinful man Thy glory may not see; Only Thou art holy; there is none beside Thee, Perfect in power, in love, and purity.

Holy, holy, holy! Lord God Almighty! All Thy works shall praise Thy Name, in earth, and sky, and sea; Holy, holy, holy; merciful and mighty! God in three Persons, blessed Trinity!

Mr. Heber wrote this hymn – Holy, Holy, Holy - for Trinity Sunday while he was Vicar of Hodnet, Shropshire, England.

In regards to the Holy Trinity, it is the mark of a Christian to accept God's Word as written, which clearly avows this teaching. God is comprised of the Father, Son, and Holy Spirit. As a Christian, if you have doubts or questions concerning this fundamental truth, you should pray and ask God to open His Word to you.

CHAPTER 4

About Baptism

Oh, worship the LORD in the beauty of holiness!
Tremble before Him, all the earth.

Psalm 96:9

Is water baptism required for salvation? In what manner should I be baptized? I was sprinkled as an infant, is that good enough?

It's amazing to see how many people get the issue of baptism so wrong and the reasons for their misunderstandings. Mostly, people just accept what their denomination teaches regardless of what the Holy Bible actually has to say about it. Baptism goes back long before the Christian era in the nation of Israel. It was practiced by full immersion. John the Baptist baptized in the Jordan and our Lord was certainly fully immersed in His baptism as mentioned in the Gospels.

Is water baptism required for salvation?

Depending on the church you attend, this and the other questions concerning baptism will certainly be answered differently. I've researched each stand on the matter and will give you what I feel is the most logical answer based on Scriptural evidence. That is, with the exception of whether baptism is required for salvation. If you attend the Church of Christ, their answer is an emphatic "yes" you must be baptized in order to be saved. Two points on this:

(1) They are basing their conclusion on these verses:

He who believes and is baptized will be saved; but he who does not believe will be condemned.

Mark 16:16

Then Peter said to them, "Repent, and let every one of you be baptized in the name of Jesus Christ for the remission of sins; and you shall receive the gift of the Holy Spirit.

Acts 2:38

(2) They are wrong.

First, baptism is a work, and the Holy Bible is very clear that no works are required for salvation. It is faith alone by which man is saved:

For by grace you have been saved through faith, and that not of yourselves; *it is* **the gift of God, not of works, lest anyone should boast.**

Ephesians 2:8, 9

I've said elsewhere that Scripture never contradicts itself and this is absolutely true. Therefore, faith in the finished work of Jesus Christ is our only requirement for salvation. The verse above and many others state this emphatically. In fact, adding anything to such faith is in essence saying that His work and His shed blood is insufficient for our justification. If this is true, we are still without hope in the world, because we can never know at what point we have done enough to complete the process. Additionally, it is saying God's plan of redemption was incompetent.

A simple Scriptural account proves salvation apart from baptism:

> **But the other, answering, rebuked him, saying, "Do you not even fear God, seeing you are under the same condemnation? And we indeed justly, for we receive the due reward of our deeds; but this Man has done nothing wrong." Then he said to Jesus, "Lord, remember me when You come into Your kingdom." And Jesus said to him, "Assuredly, I say to you, today you will be with Me in Paradise."**
>
> **Luke 23:40-43**

This criminal repented on the cross next to Jesus. He was not baptized, nor did he hand out tracks at Wal-Mart. No! Simply by faith in what Jesus was in the very process of doing, he was given the promise. By his faith, he became the first person to die after our Lord who would enter the Kingdom! What an honor, and no baptism was involved.

Concerning **Mark 16:16** above – here are John the Baptist's words concerning the baptism Jesus would provide:

> **I indeed baptized you with water, but He will baptize you with the Holy Spirit.**
>
> **Mark 1:8**

As you can see, the baptism Christ Jesus provides is a spiritual baptism. John's baptism was a baptism of repentance:

> **And he said to them, "Into what then were you baptized?" So they said, "Into John's baptism." Then Paul said, "John indeed baptized with a baptism of repentance, saying to the people that they should believe on Him who would come after him, that is, on Christ Jesus."**
>
> **Acts 19:3, 4**

It's obvious from this verse and many others, that even though John's baptism was one of repentance, early believers were still baptized in water. However, to prove the point that believers are saved by faith and receive the true baptism of the Holy Spirit at the moment of acceptance, not based on an external rite, many verses are provided. In the following account, the Holy Spirit came visibly and with signs at the moment of belief, before the converts were baptized:

> **While Peter was still speaking these words, the Holy Spirit fell upon all those who heard the word. And those of the circumcision who believed were astonished, as many as came with Peter, because the gift of the Holy Spirit had been poured out on the Gentiles also. For they heard them speak with tongues and magnify God. Then Peter answered, "Can anyone forbid water, that these should not be baptized who have received the Holy Spirit just as we *have?*" And he commanded them to be baptized in the name of the Lord. Then they asked him to stay a few days.**
>
> **Acts 10:44-48**

Paul also made the point on several occasions of indicating the seal of the Holy Spirit upon believers at the moment of belief:

> **In Him you also *trusted,* after you heard the word of truth, the gospel of your salvation; in whom also, having believed, you were sealed with the Holy Spirit of promise, who is the guarantee of our inheritance until the redemption of the purchased possession, to the praise of His glory.**
>
> **Ephesians 1:13, 14**

> **And do not grieve the Holy Spirit of God, by whom you were sealed for the day of redemption.**
>
> **Ephesians 4:30**

Concerning **Acts 2:38** (previously cited) which is used to "prove" water baptism is a requirement for salvation, we need to study the intent of the passage. In Greek, there are many words translated "for." In the case above, the word is *"eis."* Strong's Exhaustive Concordance gives many possible translations of "eis," and by taking the issue in proper context we must come to the conclusion that "for" signifies a past action. As an example, I could say that police want me for theft. This could really be taken one of two ways – I am wanted to commit a theft, or I am wanted for having committed a theft. Obviously the second makes sense based on the use of "police" and "theft" in the same sentence. It is the same with the Bible. Were it not so, there would be a contradiction on other teachings of salvation by grace alone. Rather, Christ's true baptism of the Holy Spirit comes upon acceptance of Christ's finished work.

Some denominations have a joke belittling Baptists for insisting baptism is not a requirement for salvation:

"We'll take care of the Baptists with an axe and two 38's." Or if taken literally, an **Acts** and **2:38**'s.

Actually, it's not a very funny way to joke about other blood-bought Christians, and ultimately, their stand is wholly unfounded in Scriptural truth. I would ask them when they consider such a stab at their fellow Christians to remember Paul's words (underlined for emphasis):

But fornication and all uncleanness or covetousness, let it not even be named among you, as is fitting for saints; neither filthiness, nor foolish talking, <u>nor coarse jesting,</u> which are not fitting, but rather giving of thanks.
Ephesians 5:3, 4

So the answer to the first question in this section is "no." Water baptism is not a requirement for salvation.

<u>In what manner should I be baptized?</u>
<u>Is being sprinkled as an infant acceptable?</u>
I've combined these questions into this one section simply because they belong together. The reason for this is that an explana-

tion of what water baptism symbolizes will clarify them both. Once we understand that, we can then clearly understand the answer to these two questions.

As baptism is not required for salvation (this is a certainty) and we are sealed, or "baptized" with the Holy Spirit at the moment we trusted Jesus, then there must be a different reason altogether for baptism in water. I believe the clearest answer in all Scripture can be found in the following three passages:

> **Or do you not know that as many of us as were baptized into Christ Jesus were baptized into His death? Therefore we were buried with Him through baptism into death, that just as Christ was raised from the dead by the glory of the Father, even so we also should walk in newness of life.**
>
> **Romans 6:3, 4**

> **Moreover, brethren, I do not want you to be unaware that all our fathers were under the cloud, all passed through the sea, all were baptized into Moses in the cloud and in the sea, all ate the same spiritual food, and all drank the same spiritual drink. For they drank of that spiritual Rock that followed them, and that Rock was Christ. But with most of them God was not well pleased, for *their bodies* were scattered in the wilderness.**
>
> **1 Corinthians 10:1-5**

> **In Him you were also circumcised with the circumcision made without hands, by putting off the body of the sins of the flesh, by the circumcision of Christ, buried with Him in baptism, in which you also were raised with *Him* through faith in the working of God, who raised Him from the dead. And you, being dead in your trespasses and the uncircumcision of your flesh, He has made alive together with Him, having forgiven you all trespasses,**
>
> **Colossians 2:11-13**

Here we see that we are baptized into His death. Additionally, we are raised with Him through faith in the working of God (an action of the Holy Spirit.) Water baptism, therefore, is a picture or better *identification* with the death, burial, and resurrection of the Lord Jesus. Just as Jesus died and was buried, so we are immersed in water - complete immersion. This is a picture of our death to sin; our burial with Him; and when we pop up from the water, our resurrection with Him. Just as the Old Testament Exodus account of the cloud and the sea *pictures* the actions of the coming Redeemer as mentioned above, so we complete the picture in our walk with the Lord – identifying completely with Him – by full-immersion baptism. I need not go into any more depth or argumentation than this. It is clear, concise, and a simple matter when taken in proper Biblical context.

As for sprinkling at infancy, this is a tradition – one that goes well back to antiquity – but it is none-the-less a tradition. It finds no support at all Biblically. As salvation is a personal choice, made by faith in Christ's finished work of the Cross, such a baptism is actually pointless except for the good feelings of the congregation and nice for pictures to hang on the wall by the proud parents. Confirmation in a church is similar, it's a piece of paper without substance. I agree with the need to raise children Biblically and get them involved in both the local church and its activities, but people tend to put way too much value on the externals, when it is the heart and the *intent* that the Lord will judge us by.

It is with certainty that if you read Biblical commentaries, you're going to find opposing voices on the matter of sprinkling, but the fact remains that there is no *identification* with the Lord's death, burial, and resurrection in this type of baptism. Pictures are obviously very important to the Lord's purposes as we can see throughout the Old Testament. Because of the high value to the Lord of such pictures, and personal identification with Him in His burial, I feel the best and most Christ-honoring method of baptism is that of full immersion.

Baptism bonus section!
Good feeling, but useless -

One day while watching a prominent Texas pastor, a Christian television personality, he went through the different terminologies for baptism in the Holy Bible. He mentioned baptism of this and baptism of that. One of the baptisms he mentioned was the Baptism of the Holy Spirit. At the end of the discourse, he asked the congregation that if they had never been baptized into the Holy Spirit, but only via water baptism, to come forward and receive the "Baptism of the Holy Spirit." A bunch of people came up front and the pastor held out his hands and, in his usual authoritative manner, claimed to baptize these folks into the Holy Spirit. As quoted above and again here for your reference, we receive the Holy Spirit at the moment we trust Jesus. This does not occur when a Texas preacher holds out his hands and says it is going to happen.

In Him you also *trusted,* after you heard the word of truth, the gospel of your salvation; in whom also, having believed, you were sealed with the Holy Spirit of promise, who is the guarantee of our inheritance until the redemption of the purchased possession, to the praise of His glory.

Ephesians 1:13, 14

There is no reason to do something unbiblical just because it feels good.

If you instruct the brethren in these things, you will be a good minister of Jesus Christ, nourished in the words of faith and of the good doctrine which you have carefully followed.

1 Timothy 4:6

Fun Fact: **Acts** chapter **21** ends in mid sentence with a comma in the NKJV and a colon in some other versions. It's little things like this that, to me, prove the inspiration of the Bible, right down to it's numbering.

Concerning baptism, the mark of a Christian is to put all of one's hope, trust, and faith in the finished work of Jesus Christ. According to Scripture, the moment a believer openly confesses his sinful nature and accepts Christ Jesus, he or she is marked with the Holy Spirit. As a means of identification with Jesus in His death, burial, and resurrection, believers are baptized, preferably by full immersion. This also signifies the cleansing from sin that Jesus Christ provides. However, one will not "lose" his or her salvation if they are not baptized.

CHAPTER 5

A Day to Honor the Lord

Who *is* like You, glorious in holiness, Fearful in praises, doing wonders?

Exodus 15:11

The day for Christians to observe a Sabbath or rather Worship to the Lord is actually an interesting question that can lead people into cults or the acceptance of false teachings. As this is a question that Paul dealt with on several occasions, and due to the introduction of really misleading ideas, it would be of value to go through this topic in limited detail. Areas of this page may seem difficult to understand, but with study and contemplation, I think you'll agree with the ultimate conclusion.

The first time a rest is mentioned in the Bible is in **Genesis 2:2, 3**:

And on the seventh day God ended His work which He had done, and He rested on the seventh day from all His work which He had done. Then God blessed the seventh day and sanctified it, because in it He rested from all His work which God had created and made.

When we consider this, it's evident that God did not cease all of His activities. If He did, the universe would cease to exist because it says elsewhere in Scripture that: **And *he* is before all, and all things subsist together by him. Colossians 1:17** (Darby) It was on the seventh day that God no longer performed the previous work of creation. Additionally, unlike the first 6 days, the 7th does not mention a morning or an evening. This 7th day (Sabbath) rest, which is described in **Hebrews 4:3-11** below, is eternal. Those who have accepted Christ's finished work at Calvary have entered that rest and are living in it, day by day. Here is the promise of rest for God's people:

> **For we who have believed do enter that rest, as He has said:** *" So I swore in My wrath, ' They shall not enter My rest,'"***although the works were finished from the foundation of the world. For He has spoken in a certain place of the seventh** *day* **in this way:** *"And God rested on the seventh day from all His works"***; and again in this** *place:* *"They shall not enter My rest."* **Since therefore it remains that some** *must* **enter it, and those to whom it was first preached did not enter because of disobedience, again He designates a certain day, saying in David,** *"Today,"* **after such a long time, as it has been said:** *" Today, if you will hear His voice, Do not harden your hearts."*

> **For if Joshua had given them rest, then He would not afterward have spoken of another day. There remains therefore a rest for the people of God. For he who has entered His rest has himself also ceased from his works as God** *did* **from His. Let us therefore be diligent to enter that rest, lest anyone fall according to the same example of disobedience.**

If you notice the first sentence says: **For we who have believed do enter that rest …**

This is the final point of rest and clearly indicates that a believer in the finished work of Christ Jesus is now in the promised rest and

"has himself also ceased from his works." *He is living in the 7th day Sabbath rest.*

From here, I'll try to refocus on why there was a change to Sunday worship rather than continuing with it on Saturday. But before I do, it still seems necessary to explain why the Saturday Sabbath was given to the Jewish nation, and why we don't have to follow this requirement. The Bible very clearly states that it was given to the Israelites in the Mosaic Covenant as a sign:

> **"Speak also to the children of Israel, saying: 'Surely My Sabbaths you shall keep, for it *is* a sign between Me and you throughout your generations, that *you* may know that I *am* the LORD who sanctifies you.'"**
> **Exodus 31:13.**

This is mentioned elsewhere in Scripture and is very specific, it was to be a sign between God and the Israelites. In contrast, when the gentiles were grafted into the commonwealth of Israel, there was much debate as to what requirements would be levied on them as a body. These requirements are summed up in **Acts 15:19-20**:

> **Therefore I judge that we should not trouble those from among the Gentiles who are turning to God, but that we write to them to abstain from things polluted by idols, from sexual immorality, from things strangled, and from blood.**

Later, after the initial letter from the church in Jerusalem, Paul (the apostle to the gentiles) expounded on what was required of gentiles:

> **Do you not know that the unrighteous will not inherit the kingdom of God? Do not be deceived. Neither fornicators, nor idolaters, nor adulterers, nor homosexuals, nor sodomites, nor thieves, nor covetous, nor drunkards, nor revilers, nor extortioners will inherit the kingdom of God.**
> **1 Corinthians 6:9-10**

> **Now the works of the flesh are evident, which are: adultery, fornication, uncleanness, lewdness, idolatry, sorcery, hatred, contentions, jealousies, outbursts of wrath, selfish ambitions, dissensions, heresies, envy, murders, drunkenness, revelries, and the like; of which I tell you beforehand, just as I also told *you* in time past, that those who practice such things will not inherit the kingdom of God.**
>
> **Galatians 5:19-21**

At no time were the gentile believers instructed to observe a Sabbath, and this even after they had received the Holy Spirit and been baptized. In fact, the directions given in **Acts** mentioned above very closely resemble those given to Noah after the Flood:

> **Every moving thing that lives shall be food for you. I have given you all things, even as the green herbs. But you shall not eat flesh with its life, *that is,* its blood. Surely for your lifeblood I will demand *a reckoning;* from the hand of every beast I will require it, and from the hand of man. From the hand of every man's brother I will require the life of man.**
>
> **Genesis 9:3-5**

This means that those people considered righteous by God, both before and after the Flood – Abel, Enoch, Noah, Abraham, Isaac, Israel, Levi, and Moses (until the Mosaic Covenant), etc. – were never asked to observe a Sabbath. Taking Abraham as an example, it says in **Galatians 3:6-9**:

> **...just as Abraham *"believed God, and it was accounted to him for righteousness."* Therefore know that *only* those who are of faith are sons of Abraham. And the Scripture, foreseeing that God would justify the Gentiles by faith, preached the gospel to Abraham beforehand, *saying, "In you all the nations shall be blessed."* So then those who *are* of faith are blessed with believing Abraham.**

So now we see that Abraham was considered righteous through faith and not works. If we receive the same blessing by Christ and then are considered unrighteous because of a failure to observe a Sabbath, then there is no consideration of righteousness!

Again, considering the gentiles, other than when Paul went to discuss Christ in the Jewish synagogues with gentiles in attendance, it is a Sunday, not a Saturday on which they met, and this in honor of the glorious resurrection of the Lord.

Note: If you've been taught that Christ rose on a Saturday, you were misled on this. Both the Old and New Testaments and non-biblical sources show plainly that Christ rose on Sunday morning. Christ was crucified and buried on a Friday and rose on Sunday morning. Some people get very bent out of shape over this issue because of the verbiage Jesus used in **Matthew 12:40**. However, there is no inconsistency when one realizes that in Hebrew thinking one day is considered a day when 1 hour or 24 hours is mentioned. Any part of a day therefore meets the requirements of a "day and a night."

Just to clear this up, though, I'll go through a very short testimony of a "3rd Day" Resurrection.

Leviticus 23 mandates each Feast of the Lord. For the Passover it says:

> 'These *are* the feasts of the LORD, holy convocations which you shall proclaim at their appointed times. On the fourteenth *day* of the first month at twilight *is* the LORD's Passover. And on the fifteenth day of the same month *is* the Feast of Unleavened Bread to the LORD; seven days you must eat unleavened bread.
> **Leviticus 23:4-6**

For the Feast of Firstfruits it says:

> And the LORD spoke to Moses, saying, "Speak to the children of Israel, and say to them: 'When you come into the land which I give to you, and reap its harvest, then you shall bring a sheaf of the firstfruits of your harvest to

the priest. He shall wave the sheaf before the LORD, to be accepted on your behalf; on the day after the Sabbath the priest shall wave it.

Leviticus 23:9-11

Finally, to know with a certainty what day Firstfruits was celebrated, we turn to the writing of Flavius Josephus. This man was a Jew who lived around the time of Jesus, and his writings cover the entire history of the Jewish people. The writings of Josephus provide insights into many Bible passages, from Genesis to the Diaspora. They are considered an invaluable resource for the serious student of the Bible because of the depth of information they provide. Here he clearly gives us the information we need to fill in the final blanks:

In the month of Xanthicus, which is by us called Nisan, and is the beginning of our year, on the fourteenth day of the lunar month, when the sun is in Aries, (for in this month it was that we were delivered from bondage under the Egyptians,) the law ordained that we should every year slay that sacrifice which I before told you we slew when we came out of Egypt, and which was called the Passover; and so we do celebrate this passover in companies, leaving nothing of what we sacrifice till the day following. The feast of unleavened bread succeeds that of the passover, and falls on the fifteenth day of the month, and continues seven days, wherein they feed on unleavened bread; on every one of which days two bulls are killed, and one ram, and seven lambs. Now these lambs are entirely burnt, besides the kid of the goats which is added to all the rest, for sins; for it is intended as a feast for the priest on every one of those days. But on the second day of unleavened bread, which is the sixteenth day of the month, they first partake of the fruits of the earth, for before that day they do not touch them. And while they suppose it proper to honor God, from whom they obtain this plentiful provision, in the first place, they offer the first-fruits of their barley, and that in the manner following: They take a handful of the ears, and dry them, then beat them small, and purge the barley from the bran; they then bring one tenth deal to the altar, to God; and, casting one handful of it upon the fire, they leave the rest for the use of the priest. And after this it is that they may publicly or privately reap their harvest. They also at this participation of the first-fruits of the earth, sacrifice a lamb, as a burnt-offering to God. Flavius Josephus, Antiquities, Book III Chapter 10.5

The Bible is very clear that Jesus was crucified as the Passover Lamb on the day of Passover (the 14th of the month of Nisan.) This was foreshadowed in **Leviticus 23:5** above. Josephus, being an eyewitness to the annual pilgrimage and celebration of Passover/ Unleavened Bread, says the celebration of Firstfruits occurred *on* the 3rd Day after Passover, which is the 16th of Nisan. Firstfruits was a picture of the coming resurrection as testified by Paul:

But now Christ is risen from the dead, *and* has become the firstfruits of those who have fallen asleep.
1 Corinthians 15:20

In addition to this, the term "3rd day" or "on the third day" is used 13 times in reference to the resurrection. Here is just one of them:

Him God raised up on the third day, and showed Him openly, 41 not to all the people, but to witnesses chosen before by God, *even* to us who ate and drank with Him after He arose from the dead.
Acts 10:40, 41

As with all the Feasts of the LORD, they find their fulfillment in Jesus Christ. Many have mistaken these as Jewish Feasts but the Bible never says this. It openly states that they are the Feasts of the LORD and Paul confirms that they have found fulfillment in Jesus:

So let no one judge you in food or in drink, or regarding a festival or a new moon or sabbaths, which are a shadow of things to come, but the substance is of Christ.

Colossians 2:16, 17

It may seem a little overwhelming going through so many verses to make the point, but these issues are most important in correcting erroneous doctrine, particularly with some large denominations, including the 7th Day Adventists, as well as many fringe elements. So now - concerning Sunday get-togethers:

Now on the first *day* of the week, when the disciples came together to break bread, Paul, ready to depart the next day, spoke to them and continued his message until midnight.

Acts 20:7

On the first *day* of the week let each one of you lay something aside, storing up as he may prosper, that there be no collections when I come.

1 Corinthians 16:2

Early non-biblical records definitely indicate that Sunday became the day of worship for Christians, and this in honor of the Risen Christ. Many of these documents are available on various websites and which you can read by doing a general search. Here are some of these ancient witnesses:

The first century Didache, "Christian Assembly on the Lord's Day"
The writings of Justin Martyr
The second century letter of Pliny to Trajan
The letter of Barnabas 15:6-8, written in A.D. 74
The writings of Ignatius, the bishop of Antioch, c. A.D. 115

A logical line of reasoning justifying Sunday worship and a departure from the Sabbath mandated in the Ten Commandments was brought to my attention while reading the Wycliffe Bible Commentary. First, the pertinent verses:

> **Remember the Sabbath day, to keep it holy. Six days you shall labor and do all your work, but the seventh day** *is* **the Sabbath of the LORD your God.** *In it* **you shall do no work: you, nor your son, nor your daughter, nor your male servant, nor your female servant, nor your cattle, nor your stranger who** *is* **within your gates. For** *in* **six days the LORD made the heavens and the earth, the sea, and all that** *is* **in them, and rested the seventh day. Therefore the LORD blessed the Sabbath day and hallowed it.**
>
> **Exodus 20:8-11**

> **Observe the Sabbath day, to keep it holy, as the LORD your God commanded you. Six days you shall labor and do all your work, but the seventh day** *is* **the Sabbath of the LORD your God.** *In it* **you shall do no work: you, nor your son, nor your daughter, nor your male servant, nor your female servant, nor your ox, nor your donkey, nor any of your cattle, nor your stranger who** *is* **within your gates, that your male servant and your female servant may rest as well as you. And remember that you were a slave in the land of Egypt, and the LORD your God brought you out from there by a mighty hand and by an outstretched arm; therefore the LORD your God commanded you to keep the Sabbath day.**
>
> **Deuteronomy 5:12-15**

Their well stated reason was that the variation in these two passages shows two different concepts for the Sabbath. The first in **Exodus** is based on the Creation account and says:

> **For** *in* **six days the LORD made the heavens and the earth, the sea, and all that** *is* **in them, and rested the seventh day.**

The second in **Deuteronomy** is based on the consummation of redemption and the promise of entering His rest. **And remember that you were a slave in the land of Egypt, and the LORD your God brought you out from there by a mighty hand and by an outstretched arm;**.... Actually, this was most insightful and I'm grateful for the wealth of knowledge their commentary provided, including this nugget. Because this redemption was a picture of the coming true Redemption provided by Jesus Christ and the corresponding eternal rest mentioned in **Hebrews 4:3**, as Christians we are *living in* our Sabbath rest.

It's argued among some cults and legalistic churches that Sunday worship came from:

(1) A worship of the sun.

(2) The traditions of the Roman Catholics.

Neither of these is true and neither can be supported through historical records. Rather, the overwhelming evidence is that the earliest Christians felt no obligation to observe a Sabbath because of the letter from the Council in Jerusalem. Instead they celebrated a day of worship. Several statements made by Paul back this up:

> **So let no one judge you in food or in drink, or regarding a festival or a new moon or sabbaths, which are a shadow of things to come, but the substance is of Christ.**
> **Colossians 2:16, 17**

&

> **But now after you have known God, or rather are known by God, how *is it that* you turn again to the weak and beggarly elements, to which you desire again to be in bondage? You observe days and months and seasons and years. I am afraid for you, lest I have labored for you in vain.**
> **Galatians 4:9-11**

Another most interesting point concerning this issue is that the Sabbath is the only one of the Ten Commandments not specifically mentioned as required or expounded upon in the New Testament. Further, when asked a very specific question, Jesus Himself left it out:

Now as He was going out on the road, one came running, knelt before Him, and asked Him, "Good Teacher, what shall I do that I may inherit eternal life?" So Jesus said to him, "Why do you call Me good? No one *is* good but One, *that is,* God. You know the commandments: *'Do not commit adultery,' 'Do not murder,' 'Do not steal,' 'Do not bear false witness,'* 'Do not defraud,' *'Honor your father and your mother.'"*

Mark 10:17-19 also found in **Luke 18**

I find it highly unlikely that if this were such a grave issue in the Dispensation of Grace soon to come that:

(1) Our Lord would fail to state it somewhere in His earthly ministry.

(2) It is never even remotely considered in the rest of the New Testament except as can be construed in a rather negative light by Paul.

As stated above concerning the Feasts of the LORD in **Leviticus 23,** each is specifically fulfilled in Christ. The Sabbath is the first one mentioned and its fulfillment is listed in the New Testament, specifically **Hebrews 4,** but also by Jesus' own words:

Come to Me, all *you* who labor and are heavy laden, and I will give you rest. Take My yoke upon you and learn from Me, for I am gentle and lowly in heart, and you will find rest for your souls.

Matthew 11:28, 29

Right after Jesus said this, Matthew mentions the Sabbath "at that time." Therefore, we can make the assertion that Jesus said this the same day – a Sabbath!

I do suppose that even after this short discussion, if you were originally indoctrinated into believing in a Saturday Sabbath requirement you'll never concede your point. However, the Old and New Testaments clearly demonstrate our rest is in the Lord Jesus and His finished work. Further, extra-biblical early Church records confirm that since the resurrection of our Lord, we have honored Him with a day of worship on Sunday. My belief is that it is both proper and honoring to set aside a day to worship Him. If you do this on a Saturday or a Sunday becomes a personal choice. If it's done as a sense of obligation because of the group you attend though, I believe you've fallen from the grace bestowed upon us at the Cross of Calvary.

On this issue, I leave you with a quote from **Philippians 3:15**:

Therefore let us, as many as are mature, have this mind; and if in anything you think otherwise, God will reveal even this to you.

This is the day the Lord hath made;
He calls the hours His own;
Let heav'n rejoice, let earth be glad,
And praise surround the throne.
Today He rose and left the dead,
And Satan's empire fell;
Today the saints His triumphs spread,
And all His wonders tell.
Hosanna to th'anointed King,
To David's holy Son;
Help us, O Lord; descend and bring
Salvation from Thy throne.
Blest be the Lord, Who comes to men
With messages of grace;
Who comes in God His Father's Name,
To save our sinful race.
Hosanna in the highest strains

The Church on earth can raise;
The highest heav'ns, in which He reigns,
Shall give Him nobler praise.

<u>This Is the Day the Lord Hath Made</u> was written by Isaac Watts in 1719. Isaac Watts understood that each day is a day from the Lord and a day to honor the Lord.

Concerning worship, the mark of a Christian is to worship in "Spirit and in Truth." We are to think on the Lord Jesus day and night, show our gratitude to Him for all good things, and set aside a special time where we can contemplate Him and worship with other blood-bought believers.

CHAPTER 6

Concerning Prayer

Hear my prayer, O Lord, Give ear to my supplications!

Psalm 143:1

Prayer is an integral part of the Christian life. By it we *praise* our Creator. Truly He is worthy of adoration:

"Blessing and honor and glory and power
Be to Him who sits on the throne,
And to the Lamb, forever and ever!"

Revelation 5:13

A prayer of *thanksgiving* demonstrates an understanding that,

Every good gift and every perfect gift is from above, and comes down from the Father of lights, with whom there is no variation or shadow of turning.

James 1:17

Enter into His gates with thanksgiving, *And* **into His courts with praise. Be thankful to Him,** *and* **bless His name.**

Psalm 110:4

A prayer of *confession* acknowledges that we've violated God's standards. One of the most moving prayers of confession in all Scripture is **Psalm 51**.

For I acknowledge my transgressions, And my sin *is* **always before me. Against You, You only, have I sinned, And done** *this* **evil in Your sight— That You may be found just when You speak,** *And* **blameless when You judge.**

Psalm 51:3, 4

A prayer of *petition* or *supplication* makes known to God our heart's desire. Although we don't know Hannah's words in **1 Samuel 1:13**, we do know the depth of anguish in her soul from **verse 15** -

But Hannah answered and said, "No, my lord, I *am* **a woman of sorrowful spirit.**

We also know her petition was granted by a gracious and loving God who hears.

By prayer of *acceptance of Jesus Christ*, we receive son-ship and eternal life. If you've never made such a prayer, what on earth are you waiting for? At the end of this chapter is a prayer you can use, right now, to enter into a relationship with Jesus. Don't put that off, but rather skip ahead and make a commitment now!

The Holy Bible is really clear in procedures for proper prayer. Despite what's taught by the Roman Catholic Church, there is no justification anywhere in Holy Writ to authorize prayer to or through anyone but God. When asked by his disciples how to pray, Jesus quoted the Lord's Prayer. This is the model on which we should base all prayers. I typed a short and easy to understand explanation of this prayer for the children in my Sunday school class. Here it is for you:

In this manner, therefore, pray:
Our Father in heaven,
Hallowed be Your name.
Your kingdom come.
Your will be done
On earth as *it is* in heaven.
Give us this day our daily bread.
And forgive us our debts,
As we forgive our debtors.
And do not lead us into temptation,
But deliver us from the evil one.
For Yours is the kingdom and the power
and the glory forever. Amen.

Matthew 6:9-13

Jesus told us to pray to our Father. God is called the father of Christians because through Jesus we have been lifted to an especially close and intimate relationship with Him. We should not fear Him as a stern judge, but revere him as a loving Father.

First - we must bring our honor and praise to Him.

Second - we should ask and believe that His kingdom will come. We know that this will happen when Jesus returns…just as He promised!

Third – in prayer we should again honor God by asking that His will for our lives is done, not our will. He created us, and His will is more important than ours. His will is done in heaven, but right now it's not being done on earth. There is sin and hatred and sadness here. We should always pray for Jesus to come and make this earth right!

Fourth - only after we have praised Him and asked for His will to be done in our lives should we ask for any favor. But now it's time! We can ask him to give us our daily bread. Don't forget to pray for your family and for your friends!!!

Fifth - Oops…we've all sinned and we all owe a debt for our sins. We need to ask God to now forgive us for the wrong things we've done. We confess that we haven't been the best in our hearts, in our minds, and in our actions. But make sure that you have forgiven everyone else first. See, it says, "as we forgive our debtors." Why should God forgive us if we don't forgive others first!!!!!

Sixth – We need to ask God to make us strong and keep us from temptation! We are weak, but in Jesus we can be strong. Ask God today and everyday to help you to be strong! When someone offers you drugs or asks you to steal or some other bad thing, make sure you don't! Instead ask God to help you. Remember if you have Jesus as your Savior, God is your dad. Talk to him all the time just like you would talk to your own father.

Seventh – Ask God to deliver you from the evil one – the devil. We are weak, but in Jesus we are more than strong. Yes, we can never fail if we keep our eyes on Jesus! Here is a great thing to remember - **....looking unto Jesus.... Hebrews 12:2**

Eighth – We again praise God by acknowledging that His is the Kingdom, the Power, and the Glory. We are small and helpless, but He is strong and can handle all our problems if we put Him first!!!

Just so you know …. Amen comes from the Hebrew language. It means, "So be it" or "truth" and is correctly pronounced "ahmayn."

Paul gives further advice concerning proper prayer procedures. As this is directly from our life's guide, the Canon of Scripture, and summarizes proper prayer after our Lord's resurrection and ascension, we need to remember this as a pattern for our prayer life:

Be anxious for nothing, but in everything by prayer and supplication, with thanksgiving, let your requests be made known to God; and the peace of God, which surpasses all understanding, will guard your hearts and minds through Christ Jesus.

Philippians 4:6, 7

The term "through" is used again and again by Paul as he weaves it into the very fabric of what prayer should resemble. In **1 Timothy 2:5,** Paul says:

For *there is* one God and one Mediator between God and men, *the* Man Christ Jesus.

This tells us that in order to connect with God, we cannot do it through a priest, a church, a pope, Mary, Buddha, Krishna, a satellite dish, a frog, or by any other means. Jesus Christ is our appointed Mediator and it is through Him alone that our prayers will be acknowledged.

George Washington, the first President of The United States, understood this principle:

Almighty God, we make our earnest prayer that Thou wilt keep the United States in thy holy protection, that Thou wilt incline the hearts of the citizens to cultivate a spirit of subordination and obedience to government, and entertain a brotherly affection and love for one another and for their fellow citizens of the United States at large. And finally that Thou wilt most graciously be pleased to dispose us all to do justice, to love mercy, and to demean ourselves with that charity, humility, and pacific temper of mind which were the characteristics of the Divine Author of our blessed religion, and without a humble imitation of whose example in these things, we can never hope to be a happy nation. Grant our supplications, we beseech Thee, through Jesus Christ our Lord. Amen.

He understood that Jesus Christ is the sole Mediator between fallen man and Almighty God and his prayer reflects this fundamental truth.

These are important rules for the governance of our prayer, remembering that prayer truly is our method of communication with the Creator. I believe it's so important to remember that I'll restate it here - God hears all prayer, or He is not omniscient. However, prayer not conducted *through* Jesus is wasting one's breath. No prayer...No prayer at all is acceptable to God unless it is preceded by faith. As it says in **Hebrews 11:6**:

But without faith *it is* impossible to please *Him,* for he who comes to God must believe that He is, and *that* He is a rewarder of those who diligently seek Him.

And what faith is Paul indicating? Faith in what God has done *through* Jesus Christ. Therefore, without faith in the finished work of Jesus Christ, the prayer is unacceptable to God. If you're not praying to God through Jesus, just pray to your TV or a barbecue grill - they'll listen and respond as readily as God will. Because of our inherit sin-nature, the Bible requires our sins to be dealt with *before* our communication with God is acceptable. The book of **Hebrews** also states:

And according to the law almost all things are purified with blood, and without shedding of blood there is no remission.
Hebrews 9:22

In addition to the shedding of blood, it must be a perfect, sinless sacrifice. God Himself provided this sacrifice in the person and work of Jesus Christ. By acceptance of Christ, God imputes to us His righteousness. And the trade went both ways:

For He made Him who knew no sin *to be* sin for us, that we might become the righteousness of God in Him.
2 Corinthians 5:21

In essence, God took something of immeasurable value and traded it for what is immeasurably worthless. Why He looked to man and decided on this course, I cannot understand. However, He did - sending His Son to the cross to pay the sin-debt that you and I owe. Suffice it to say, that if God allowed one person into His heaven without that person going through Jesus, then Jesus would have died a cross-death for absolutely no reason. Jesus truly is the Way, the Truth, and the Life. By Him, we can again have a right standing with our Creator. Without Him our condemnation remains. Think! Think and act on God's great gift. To turn away from or downplay such an act is to reject the very God who holds eternity, your eternity, in His mighty grasp.

Concerning the acceptability of audible or silent prayers - this is my opinion only, but we read in **Genesis 24:45**:

"But before I had finished speaking in my heart, there was Rebekah, coming out with her pitcher on her shoulder; and she went down to the well and drew *water*. And I said to her, 'Please let me drink.'

A silent prayer was also heard by God in **1 Samuel 1:13** when Hannah prayed for a child. In both occasions, no vocalization occurred yet God heard and answered the prayer. Interestingly, the 17th letter of the Hebrew aleph-bet is the letter Pe. It is drawn in 2 ways, one with a closed mouth at the beginning or within a word, and with an open mouth (Pe soffit) at the end of a word. It's believed the closed mouth refers to speech in this world, and the open mouth to speech in the world to come. The word for mouth is Peh and is pronounced like the letter. As believers are already "crucified with Christ" and dead to this world, I'll be bold and state that true believers need not vocalize their prayers to be heard, but non-believers must vocalize a prayer. This goes along with the verse:

that if you confess with your mouth the Lord Jesus and believe in your heart that God has raised Him from the dead, you will be saved.

Romans 10:9

A prayer of confession must be audible.

Concerning prayer to dead people as is practiced in the Roman Catholic Church (RCC), this is never condoned in Scripture. Mary is dead and in her grave awaiting the return of the Lord Jesus. She is with Jesus in spirit, just as all believers who have passed on are, but without a body. Those who have died in Christ are all in this situation as confirmed by the Holy Bible:

We are confident, yes, well pleased rather to be absent from the body and to be present with the Lord.
2 Corinthians 5:8

&

For the Lord Himself will descend from heaven with a shout, with the voice of an archangel, and with the trumpet of God. And the dead in Christ will rise first. Then we who are alive *and* remain shall be caught up together with them in the clouds to meet the Lord in the air. And thus we shall always be with the Lord.
1 Thessalonians 4:16, 17

In addition to Mary, we are not to pray to or through the saints, the pope, angels, or any other created being. Only God is worthy of our prayers, either in praise or petition. The RCC has gone so far beyond Scripture that they actually condone, through the pope, the worship of idols.

As an example of the completely blasphemous statements issued by them, I ask you to go to this link:

http://www.vatican.va/roman_curia/tribunals/apost_penit/documents/rc_trib_appen_doc_20051118_decreto-immacolata_en.html

Because of copyright concerns, I won't reprint it here, as I have no intention of writing them and asking for permission for its use. However, by visiting this link, you can see for yourself just how unscriptural their worship of Mary has become. Through the pope, the RCC urges its faithful to violate Scripture by praying to the "Mother of God." This is done by *venerating an image of her* while you recite, "You are All Fair, Mary, and in you there is no stain of original sin!" Or equally as bizarre, "O Queen, conceived without original sin, pray for us!" For committing this blasphemy, the pope promises a plenary indulgence.

Christians do not pray to or through idols, and the need for plenary indulgences to expedite release from purgatory is an invention of the mind, having no basis in Scripture. Indulgences were created by the RCC for the purpose of making money. By purchasing indulgences, a person was led to believe they could shorten the time their soul, or that of a loved one, would stay in purgatory. The practice of selling indulgences no longer exists, but the giving of them out as rewards has never been discontinued. There is no reward for praying to or through idols or created beings except the reward of condemnation. It is no small matter to instruct others into hell.

The abovementioned letter is not an isolated case of the temporary failing of the papacy, but is a common sort of communication from Rome. Such an edict clearly violates the First and Second Commandments, and is therefore opposed to God. I attempt to read the notes published by the Vatican on behalf of the "pope" once a week and can assure you that items of this sort are sent out on a regular basis. You can do your own check anytime by visiting - www. vatican.va. As you scroll around the Vatican's site, you can go back in the archives by doing general or specific searches on their own search engine. It's absolutely appalling and frightful to see how far from the confines of the Holy Bible the RCC has deviated.

Purgatory schmurgatory – it doesn't exist.

Praying to Mary denies God His rightful due.

Idol worship will result in eternal condemnation.

Prayer to Mary and Marian worship is a Roman Catholic reinvention of an ancient cult - The Queen of Heaven. The Vatican has many titles for Mary, one of them being the Queen of Heaven. This ancient cult, by name, is specifically referred to in **Jeremiah** and became the singular reason for the destruction of the people who had fled to Egypt:

Thus says the LORD of hosts, the God of Israel, saying: 'You and your wives have spoken with your mouths and fulfilled with your hands, saying, "We will surely keep our vows that we have made, to burn incense to the queen of heaven and pour out drink offerings to her." You will surely keep your vows and perform your vows!'

> Therefore hear the word of the LORD, all Judah who
> dwell in the land of Egypt: 'Behold, I have sworn by
> My great name,' says the LORD, 'that My name shall
> no more be named in the mouth of any man of Judah
> in all the land of Egypt, saying, "The Lord GOD lives."
> Behold, I will watch over them for adversity and not for
> good. And all the men of Judah who *are* in the land of
> Egypt shall be consumed by the sword and by famine,
> until there is an end to them.
>
> **Jeremiah 44:25-27**

The same God who destroyed these people from His presence
will do the same to our modern Marian worshippers when the time
is right.

> **"For I am the LORD, I do not change.**
>
> **Malachi 3:6**

One general principal of the Vatican is the infallibility of the
pope and the placing of doctrine from the "Magesterium" on equal
footing with Scripture. This in essence makes the pope equal
with God, which would be laughable if it weren't such a serious
matter. Rumor has it that the miter worn by the pope actually states
"Vicarious Dei." I researched the matter and found this was only a
rumor started by the 7th Day Adventist church which is not true.
However, the actions of the RCC make it easy to believe this is their
doctrine. It really is terrible.

> **For My own sake, for My own sake, I will do it; For how
> should My name be profaned? And I will not give My
> glory to another.**
>
> **Isaiah 48:11**

God protects His glory and authority. It is no laughing matter
that people so flippantly disregard God's Word to follow their own
delusions, and surely the Vatican and the pope - who daily becomes

more aligned with the False Prophet of the book of Revelation - will be judged most severely for their anti-Biblical stands and practices.

My brethren, let not many of you become teachers, knowing that we shall receive a stricter judgment.
James 3:1

It is for these reasons, and others clearly portrayed in Scripture that I feel with confidence that the papal office is somehow tied to the mysterious MOTHER OF HARLOTS portrayed in **Revelation 17**.

Having said all that, it is not my place to judge another's heart. I've heard people so strongly condemn RCC members that they question the salvation of anyone who would presume to attend the RCC. It is not our right to judge any man's salvation when they've openly called on the name of Jesus. In the letter to Sardis, the Risen Lord speaks these comforting words:

You have a few names even in Sardis who have not defiled their garments; and they shall walk with Me in white, for they are worthy.
Revelation 3:4

Yes, there are good people in bad churches. Those who so arrogantly point fingers at other blood-bought believers fail to realize that even though one finger is pointing at the accused, three more are pointing right back at them. Scripture clearly indicates that a believer worships in spirit and in truth. The place where one worships is far less important than how their heart is towards Jesus Christ. A classic Old Testament example comes from the beautiful account of Naaman the Syrian in **2 Kings 5:18, 19**:

Yet in this thing may the LORD pardon your servant: when my master goes into the temple of Rimmon to worship there, and he leans on my hand, and I bow down in the temple of Rimmon—when I bow down in the temple of Rimmon, may the LORD please pardon

your servant in this thing." Then he said to him, "Go in peace." So he departed from him a short distance.

People!

Take heed to yourself and to the doctrine. Continue in them, for in doing this you will save both yourself and those who hear you.

1 Timothy 4:16

If you're reading this and haven't given serious thought to your prayer and worship life, you must do so. In all things related to God, unless specifically promised by Him - whether conditionally or unconditionally - *we* are under the obligation, not God. Truly it is a dreadful thing to fall into the hands of the Living God. What is your canon, the measuring rod, by which you will live? If it's merely the teaching of men, you've fallen under the same condemnation of those Jesus Himself pointed out:

He answered and said to them, "Well did Isaiah prophesy of you hypocrites, as it is written: *'This people honors Me with their lips, But their heart is far from Me. And in vain they worship Me, Teaching as doctrines the commandments of men.'*

Mark 7:6, 7

I beg you to consider these matters and carefully choose the way that leads to life and away from condemnation. As I said earlier in this section, if you've never made a personal commitment to Jesus Christ, now is the time.

Prayer is the Christian's vital breath,
The Christian's native air,
His watchword at the gates of death;
He enters heaven with prayer.
O Thou, by Whom we come to God,
The Life, the Truth, the Way;

The path of prayer Thyself hast trod:
Lord, teach us how to pray!
Prayer is the contrite sinner's voice,
Returning from his ways,
While angels in their songs rejoice
And cry, "Behold, he prays!"

These are three of the verses from the hymn <u>Prayer Is the Soul's Sincere Desire</u> written by James Montgomery in 1818.

Heavenly Father, You alone are worthy of praise and petition. Please forgive us of our insufficient prayer life, which in itself, borders on sin. We confess that our prayers fail to honor You and rather focus on our own needs. Give us the wisdom and strength to pray effectively – to Your glory, for the needs of others, and only then for that which concerns our own desires. For it is in Jesus' name we pray. Amen.

In prayer, the mark of a Christian is to glorify God by submitting our prayers to Him alone <u>through</u> Jesus Christ. A Christian will never pray to or worship a created being, thus depriving God of the honor that is solely due Him.

"God, I know I'm a sinner, I'm lost, and I need to be saved. I know I can't save myself, so right now, once and for all, I trust You to save me. Come into my heart, forgive my sin, and make me Your child. I give You my life. I will live for You as You give me strength."

If you said this prayer of faith, I rejoice with you. Please, read your Bible daily and never look back! Fix your eyes on Jesus!

CHAPTER 7

Tithing or Giving
The Law or Grace

**Every word of God *is* pure; He *is* a shield to those
who put their trust in Him.**

Proverbs 30:5

One area of preaching that will get me extremely hot under the collar is the inaccurate quoting of the tithing requirement of the Old Testament, and that in a New Testament church. In every other area, New Testament churches preach the doctrine of Grace. Ask any New Testament preacher if we are under the Law or Grace and they'll certainly tell you Grace, as it should be. However, these same men will eventually preach on the subject of tithing - an issue with no pertinent reference in the New Testament after the crucifixion except for instruction about Old Testament matters. The other times it's mentioned in the New Testament is when Jesus spoke in a negative context to the Pharisees of His day about their attitude for giving. Remember that our Lord's entire earthly ministry was under the Old Testament economy until the New Covenant was established the night before His crucifixion. Other than these references by Jesus, tithing is only mentioned in the book of **Hebrews**, and merely to explain the Old Testament system. Despite this fact, every preacher I've ever heard preach on the subject reverts from Grace to the Law.

From the Bible, direction concerning the Law versus Grace:

For the law was given through Moses, but grace and truth came through Jesus Christ.

John 1:17

Moreover the law entered that the offense might abound. But where sin abounded, grace abounded much more.

Romans 5:20

For sin shall not have dominion over you, for you are not under law but under grace.

Romans 6:14

I do not set aside the grace of God; for if righteousness comes through the law, then Christ died in vain.

Galatians 2:21

You have become estranged from Christ, you who attempt to be justified by law; you have fallen from grace.

Galatians 5:4

Just as it should be, we are to preach salvation by the grace of our Lord and His mercy through faith, not deeds of the law. This is what brings us salvation and blessing. And yet when it comes to money, all that is thrown to the wind and the law invariably gets reintroduced.

One of the most common Bible quotes that you will hear on the subject of tithing is:

Will a man rob God? Yet you have robbed Me! But you say, 'In what way have we robbed You?' In tithes and offerings.

Malachi 3:8

After this reading, you'll be given an hour sermon on how you're stealing from God if you don't give ten percent just as the Bible says. But does it? Let's quote the pertinent passages from the Old Testament concerning tithing. Read carefully, but underlining will be helpful here and is added by me. Remember, I didn't write these words – they're right in your Bible:

But *when* you cross over the Jordan and dwell in the land which the LORD your God is giving you to inherit, and He gives you rest from all your enemies round about, so that you dwell in safety, then there will be the place where the LORD your God chooses to make His name abide. There you shall bring all that I command you: your burnt offerings, your sacrifices, your tithes, the heave offerings of your hand, and all your choice offerings which you vow to the LORD. And you shall rejoice before the LORD your God, you and your sons and your daughters, your male and female servants, and the Levite who *is* within your gates, since he has no portion nor inheritance with you.

Deuteronomy 12:10-12

Only the holy things which you have, and your vowed offerings, you shall take and go to the place which the LORD chooses. And you shall offer your burnt offerings, the meat and the blood, on the altar of the LORD your God; and the blood of your sacrifices shall be poured out on the altar of the LORD your God, and <u>you</u> shall eat the meat.

Deuteronomy 12:26, 27

"You shall truly tithe all the increase of your grain that the field produces year by year. <u>And you shall eat before the LORD your God, in the place where He chooses to make His name abide, the tithe of your grain and your new wine and your oil, of the firstborn of your herds and your flocks</u>, that you may learn to fear the LORD your

95

God always. But if the journey is too long for you, so that you are not able to carry *the tithe, or* if the place where the LORD your God chooses to put His name is too far from you, when the LORD your God has blessed you, then you shall exchange *it* for money, take the money in your hand, and go to the place which the LORD your God chooses. And you shall spend that money for whatever your heart desires: for oxen or sheep, for wine or similar drink, for whatever your heart desires; you shall eat there before the LORD your God, and you shall rejoice, you and your household. You shall not forsake the Levite who *is* within your gates, for he has no part nor inheritance with you.

"At the end of *every* third year you shall bring out the tithe of your produce of that year and store *it* up within your gates. And the Levite, because he has no portion nor inheritance with you, and the stranger and the fatherless and the widow who *are* within your gates, may come and eat and be satisfied, that the LORD your God may bless you in all the work of your hand which you do.

Deuteronomy 14:22-29

"When you have finished laying aside all the tithe of your increase in the third year—the year of tithing—and have given *it* to the Levite, the stranger, the fatherless, and the widow, so that they may eat within your gates and be filled, then you shall say before the LORD your God: 'I have removed the holy *tithe* from *my* house, and also have given them to the Levite, the stranger, the fatherless, and the widow, according to all Your commandments which You have commanded me; I have not transgressed Your commandments, nor have I forgotten *them*.

Deuteronomy 26:12, 13

Come to Bethel, and transgress; at Gilgal multiply transgression; and bring your sacrifices every morning, and <u>your tithes after three years</u>.

Amos 4:4 (KJV)

In **Deuteronomy**, and for the rest of the Old Testament, tithing is mandatory, but for the first two years it is to be spent *by the one tithing* and his family in the presence of the LORD – for food, for drink, for rejoicing. Only in the third year is the tithe to be entirely given away. The only additional requirement besides spending the entire tithe on a party in the presence of the LORD for the first two years is the sentence, **"You shall not forsake the Levite who *is* within your gates, for he has no part nor inheritance with you."** I've always said that if God repeats Himself in the Bible, it's for the reason of clarity. In this case, it mentions the "third year" tithe not once, not twice, but three times. There can be no mistaking this.

I've read that because of the variation between **Deuteronomy** and the earlier tithing requirements (such as in **Leviticus**), some Jewish and Christian exegetes say the Bible actually stipulates a second or even a third tithe. I'll bet. These "exegetes" are most certainly dual-hatted synagogue rabbis or church pastors who would have to face losing approximately 67 percent of their income if they simply accepted the Bible for it's black and white lettering! Their view disregards the fact that **Deuteronomy** was written in the form of an ancient suzerainty treaty. It is the treaty by which the people of Israel would guide their lives. Anything in it that differs from the first four books of the Bible is either a replacement of that thought or a further defining of it. In other words, what is written in **Deuteronomy** concerning tithing is the standard and only further defines tithing where it is previously mentioned. Here's an example of what I mean from the Ten Commandments:

The 10th Commandment in **Deuteronomy** differs from its initial reception at Sinai:

"You shall not covet your neighbor's house; you shall not covet your neighbor's wife, nor his male servant, nor his

female servant, nor his ox, nor his donkey, nor anything that *is* your neighbor's."

Exodus 20:17

'You shall not covet your neighbor's wife; and you shall not desire your neighbor's house, his field, his male servant, his female servant, his ox, his donkey, or anything that *is* your neighbor's.'

Deuteronomy 5:21

Here a "field" is added into the commandment in **Deuteronomy**. During the wilderness wanderings, there was no ownership of property, but at the renewal of the covenant in **Deuteronomy** the change is made in anticipation of this occurrence. Likewise, regulations concerning tithing in **Deuteronomy** were the standard for Israel.

I heard one pastor on TV indicate that the "third year is a special, extra year of tithing in addition to the regular annual 10%." Never mind the fact that it NEVER says such a thing in the Bible. This is in line with the other incorrect analysis above and has absolutely no ground in the truth of what is clearly written. I've also heard it said that with the tithing and all the other required sacrifices, almost thirty percent of what an Israelite made would have been required. Again, this is simply not correct. Many of the required sacrifices were eaten by the one who brought them after the removal of the sacred portion by the priests. These arguments simply have no basis in the truth. The passages above clearly indicate that the third year tithe alone was given away in its entirety and the other two years' tithes were enjoyed by the giver in the presence of the LORD.

None of this really matters though because ALL of this train of thought comes from the law – the Old Testament. And, as cited in verses above, we are *not* under the law. The closest we can come to a general rule of thumb for giving in the New Testament is this:

Now concerning the collection for the saints, as I have given orders to the churches of Galatia, so you must do also: On the first *day* of the week let each one of you lay

98

something aside, storing up as he may prosper, that there be no collections when I come.

1 Corinthians 16:1, 2

There you have the only real direction given to any New Testament saint – lay something aside, storing up as you may prosper. The next time your pastor tells you that you're stealing from God if you don't tithe, ask him to show you the standard for tithing in the Bible. If he can find it at all, then ask him if you're under law or grace. Finally, if he still insists on an Old Testament tithe, ask why he's not instructing you to give in the Biblical fashion – every third year. In any case, he's trying to have his cake and eat it too.

I do suppose that if pastors spent more time preaching the glories of the Cross, and how Christ gave His all for us, people would appreciate more where their money was going and be willing to give out of a grateful heart and not a sense of *obligation* – which is exactly what the law demanded. Personally, I'd say 10% is a good starting point, but that we should give based on how we are reflecting appreciation to God for the immeasurable gift He gave us in the person of Jesus Christ. This attitude is clearly proclaimed in Scripture as well:

But this *I say:* He who sows sparingly will also reap sparingly, and he who sows bountifully will also reap bountifully. *So let* each one *give* as he purposes in his heart, not grudgingly or of necessity; for God loves a cheerful giver.

2 Corinthians 9:6, 7

A final point on tithing, this can be a *hindrance* as much as a benefit. I've heard of people starting out in business and giving 10%, but actually becoming so blessed that they now give 90% of their income. Counting beans so that every person gives exactly 10 percent can actually hinder giving when dealing with wealthier or more generous people. Giving in Christianity must be a matter of the heart or there is no appreciation of grace.

This is where the rubber hits the road. If a pastor or teacher reads these passages in the Bible, understands them, and continues to instruct incorrectly, they have put their personal desire for financial gain above what the Bible instructs. Error in doctrine is sin – how much worse if it is intentional!

The "to who" and why of giving...

Now that we know that there is NO mandated tithe in the New Testament, and the tithe we've been misled to believe in doesn't even exist as described, let's consider to whom and why we should give.

If you've ever watched a televangelist, you've certainly heard the words, "sow a seed." This appeals to the greedy side of the giver.

If you give, you'll be blessed.
Give and expect.
Give in faith and reap a harvest.
Etc...

This mindset almost makes me nauseous. If you're giving in order to get, you have an entirely different concept of the Christian message than the one presented in the Bible. This is not to say that God doesn't faithfully bless those who are obedient to him, but the intent of the heart concerning your gift says a lot about your ultimate relationship with your Savior. You might as well put your money in a slot machine as the result you're looking for is no different.

During the writing of this book, one of the "personalities" that daily appears on every Christian channel has been asking for his viewers to give for his new jet plane. If you give $10,000, he promises to put your name on a plaque at the front and back of his plane. If you give $1000 he'll put your name on a plaque in the back only. Then he promises to pray for you each time he passes the plaque. Put your money in the slot and wait for the payoff. If you gave to this guy you've been suckered. Why would such a person need a $6,000,000 aircraft? If he were to fly first class everyday for the rest of his life, he'd never spend that much. Adding in the costs of fuel, a personal pilot, etc., you can see how absolutely absurd his request is and what a dishonest heart he must truly have.

For the most part, televangelists are the last people I'd be willing to give to – especially if they ever promise a blessing in return; that they will pray for you; that you can expect to reap a harvest; or for any other reason. If you give, do it because the Lord of all creation hung on a tree to redeem you. He bought you back at the greatest cost of all and in gratitude you should give for the furtherance of the Gospel.

Don't you have a local church to give to? One that supports Bible-believing missionaries? Think! If you give to the Episcopal Church, you're giving to a body that promotes anti-biblical teachings, homo-sexuality among them. The same God who calls homosexuality an abomination in the Old Testament treats the matter in like fashion in the New. Before you proudly state you're a Methodist, Baptist, Catholic – or whatever – remember first your duty to Christ. If you're in a larger denomination, go on line and read their annual meeting minutes. If you have any moral compass, you may be appalled at some of the programs they're throwing at with the money God has trusted YOU to handle. Remember, when you give to an organi-zation, you are showing an active support for their policies. How do you think the Lord feels when you donate to an organization that condones the murder of unborn children, homosexuality, idol worship, or a host of other abominable issues? Think! Think! Stop and think what you are ultimately accountable to your Creator for.

Because of the negative vibes you must have received from this short chapter, I thought that just for fun I'd add in a bonus for you. The Hebrew word for "donut" is pronounced "soofganyah" and is a combination of three words, "end," "garden," and "God." Therefore, the word for donut has the basic meaning, "The end of the garden of God." Maybe it's because they're so tasty and delicious that someone thought, "Oy, we lost paradise, but this is the next best thing!"

When giving, rejoice in His goodness and give more than you can afford in gratitude for His unlimited mercy!

In giving, the mark of a Christian is to understand that all we have came from the open hand of the Creator. We are the recipients of His grace and love. Further, He sent His Son to pay our sin-debt. When you give to your church or other Christian charity, the percent of what you make is far less important than knowing that it's not enough. If so moved, give up a luxury and donate that amount along with your weekly giving. Finally, it is the mark of a Christian to ensure his money is being spent to further the Gospel of Jesus Christ and not on an immoral or greedy organization.

CHAPTER 8

Eternal Salvation

Therefore, having been justified by faith, we have peace with God through our Lord Jesus Christ.

Romans 5:1

What does it mean to be saved? Can you lose your salvation? What do you need to do to be saved?

In my words, salvation in the Bible involves man moving from death to life through the finished work of Jesus Christ. Jesus called it being "born again."

Jesus answered, "I tell you the truth, no one can enter the kingdom of God unless he is born of water and the Spirit. Flesh gives birth to flesh, but the Spirit gives birth to spirit.

John 3:5, 6

One of the simplest ways of explaining our dilemma and how to correct it is called the Romans Road. There are variants in this approach, but they all carry the same basic message to its conclusion. It's called the Romans Road because, normally, most of the verses used for the walk come from the book of **Romans**. Just as "all roads lead to Rome" indicated the importance of the city to the empire, the book of **Romans** has been called the "Constitution of Christianity" because of its central importance to understanding New Testament Christianity. Listed below are some pertinent verses from **Romans** - my version of the Romans Road - and a brief explanation for each. Feel free to use this as you witness to others:

> **There is none righteous, no, not one;**
>
> **Romans 3:10**

The Bible tells us that because we have a sin nature, we are unrighteous in God's sight.

- Don't look to your own goodness to save you.

> **...for all have sinned and fall short of the glory of God,**
>
> **Romans 3:23**

We all have sin in our hearts – it's our very nature to sin. We all were born with sin and without Jesus we are under the power of sin's control.

- Admit that you are a sinner.

> **For the wages of sin *is* death, but the gift of God *is* eternal life in Christ Jesus our Lord.**
>
> **Romans 6:23**

Sin results in death and we all face physical death, the result of sin. But worse is our spiritually dead condition that has alienated us from God. Unless we're reborn, it will last for all eternity. The Bible clearly teaches there is a place called the Lake of Fire where lost people will be in torment forever. It's the place where people who are spiritually dead will remain.

- Understand that you deserve death for your sin.

However, salvation is a gift from God to you! You can't earn this gift, instead you must reach out and receive it.

- Ask God to forgive you and save you.

But God demonstrates His own love toward us, in that while we were still sinners, Christ died for us.

Romans 5:8

When Jesus died on the cross He paid the penalty for our sin – all our sin. He bought us out of slavery to sin and death! The only requirement on our part is that we believe in Him and what He has done for us, understanding that we are given new life through Him, and that He is our life. He did all this because He loved us and gave Himself for us!

- Accept the gift! His love alone saves you — not religion, church membership, or family heritage. God loves you, and the gift is waiting!

For "whoever calls on the name of the LORD shall be saved."

Romans 10:13

Do it today! Make it known that you are standing for Christ and the Gospel.

- Call out to God in the name of Jesus!

...that if you confess with your mouth the Lord Jesus and believe in your heart that God has raised Him from the dead, you will be saved.

Romans 10:9

The term "justification" as used in the Bible is a legal term. When you call on Jesus, you stand righteous in God's eyes. You can never stand condemned again because Christ's perfect righteousness has now been imputed to you. Every sin you have ever committed or ever will commit is now under the precious blood of the spotless Lamb of God.

- You know God is knocking on your heart's door, so ask Him to come into your heart. Believe in your heart and confess it with your mouth!

After a person has gone down the Romans Road and truly decided on a commitment to Jesus Christ, Satan will sooner or later step in and try to convince him or her that the conversion wasn't real, or that they've committed some sin which will make them lose their salvation. The Good News is that this can never happen – never! As stated in the chapter on baptism, from the moment of acceptance of Jesus Christ, a person is sealed with the Holy Spirit and this will never be taken away. Neither man nor devil can overcome the power of God's Holy Spirit living in you. You have moved from death to life and the worst thing that may occur is severe chastisement by God for failing to live up to the standards that He expects, and also a terrible testimony of the Christian message.

And I give them eternal life, and they shall never perish; neither shall anyone snatch them out of My hand. My Father, who has given *them* to Me, is greater than all; and no one is able to snatch *them* out of My Father's hand.
John 10:28, 29

&

You are of God, little children, and have overcome them, because He who is in you is greater than he who is in the world.
1 John 4:4

In **Ephesians 2:8, 9** and about 20 other times in Scripture, salvation is either directly or indirectly called a "gift." A gift is something that cannot be earned. But more to the point, it is the gift of *God.*

God, unlike us, has eternal standards. In the case of giving a gift, it is an eternal gift. I've learned that the epistle to the **Ephesians** has logical divisions by the terms, "sit," "walk," and "stand." Using these three actions, I'd like to show how they demonstrate eternal salvation.

> **...and raised *us* up together, and made *us* sit together in the heavenly *places* in Christ Jesus,**
>
> **Ephesians 2:6**

We are made alive in Christ Jesus and afterwards *sit* together (completed action) with Christ Jesus. The action of sitting indicates finality, an accomplished deed. *When dinner is served....it's time to sit!*

> **For we are His workmanship, created in Christ Jesus for good works, which God prepared beforehand that we should walk in them.**
>
> **Ephesians 2:10**

This indicates the type of life we are to *walk* in Christ, "**for good works.**" The action of walking is a continuous, lifelong pursuit. Until our last a breath, we should be ever striving towards the

> **"...upward call of God in Christ Jesus."**
>
> **Philippians 3:14**

However, no mention is made of what would compromise our salvation if we failed to walk accordingly. It leaves us with the obvious question, "Just *what* would cause the loss of salvation?" In other words, you're back to living the Roman Catholic life - never knowing how much you need to do to satisfy God, praying the rosary, saying Hail Mary's, and in need of last rites. This (bad) theology renders justification by faith alone entirely without merit, and yet such justification is the principle tenet of Paul's writings. Once the pardon granted by Jesus' shed blood is accepted, a soul stands justified. It cannot be revoked without violating the promise of the One pardoning.

In chapter 6 of **Ephesians**, we are three times implored to *stand*. This indicates a defensive posture leading to a completed action, but not in the sense of accomplished salvation. Rather, it is referring to the Christian walk against the spiritual darkness of the world around us. If the term "stand" were indicative of the possibility of lost salvation, Paul would have clearly indicated so. Further, such an action would mean that the devil has the ability to overcome and negate what God has accomplished through Christ Jesus in our lives. Should that be the case, the entire message of man's redemption is rendered useless. You might as well drink till you vomit and tackle any woman you want as there is no hope. Finally, he recognizes the most important part of our defensive protection - the "helmet of salvation."

> **And take the helmet of salvation, and the sword of the Spirit, which is the word of God;**
>
> **Ephesians 6:17**

It is the crowning part of the Christian's uniform and indicates in absolute terms that we are adorned with eternal salvation. Interestingly enough, in **2 Samuel 22:36** (below) and in the **Psalms**, King David, under the law, equated salvation as a "shield."

> **You have also given me the shield of Your salvation; Your gentleness has made me great.**

It seems that salvation under the law was a different protection, anticipating Christ to come. Not until Jesus had gone to the cross did salvation truly reign in the believer, crowning him with the finished work of Christ!

To teach anything other than Once Saved, Always Saved is to completely disregard the entire focus and point of Paul's writings. As I've said elsewhere, the Holy Bible makes it very clear that Paul was Christ Jesus' personal messenger and chosen apostle to carry forward the message of salvation to the Gentiles. To reject Paul's authority and divine inspiration is to reject the Risen Christ:

But the Lord said to him, "Go, for he is a chosen vessel of Mine to bear My name before Gentiles, kings, and the children of Israel.

Acts 9:15

It is Jesus' authority and decision making power which are on trial when questioning the infallibility of Scripture or the divine inspiration of the writers.

"...knowing this first, that no prophecy of Scripture is of any private interpretation, for prophecy never came by the will of man, but holy men of God spoke *as they were* moved by the Holy Spirit."

2 Peter 1:20, 21

I implore you to think on these things, study your Bible diligently, and not get caught up in false teachings that are designed to hold you captive to the worries of this world. Jesus Christ did not come to establish a religion that holds us bondage to superstitious teachings, work-based salvation, or eternal insecurity. He came and lived the perfect life, and by faith in Him alone we are justified. As the Commander of the Lord's Army, unlike our staff officers in the military, He goes ahead of us as an example of the mighty power of the eternal Godhead.

If you've given your life to Jesus Christ, you are eternally saved. Rejoice and sing with me the wonderful words of Isaac Watts, <u>When I Survey the Wondrous Cross</u>...

When I survey the wondrous cross On which the Prince of glory died, My richest gain I count but loss, And pour contempt on all my pride.

Forbid it, Lord, that I should boast, Save in the death of Christ my God! All the vain things that charm me most, I sacrifice them to His blood.

See from His head, His hands, His feet, Sorrow and love flow mingled down! Did e'er such love and sorrow meet, Or thorns compose so rich a crown?

His dying crimson, like a robe, Spreads o'er His body on the tree; Then I am dead to all the globe, And all the globe is dead to me.

Were the whole realm of nature mine, That were a present far too small; Love so amazing, so divine, Demands my soul, my life, my all.

Isaac Watts – 1707

Fun Fact: You've probably heard that the shortest sentence in the Bible is **Jesus Wept. John 11:35**. However, in the original language, **Rejoice always. 1 Thessalonians 5:16** is shorter. Here they are in Greek from the Textus Receptus:

Edakrusen o Iesous. John 11:35
Pantote chairete. 1 Thessalonians 5:16

Concerning eternal salvation, the mark of a Christian is to accept the Biblical teaching of justification by faith alone and that once this occurs, the believer is eternally secure and free from condemnation. Christians understand that the power of God is more powerful than that of the devil. True Christians can loudly proclaim – "Whoo hoo! I'm saved!"

CHAPTER 9

Grace, Grace – God's Grace!

The grace of our Lord Jesus Christ be with you all. Amen.

Revelation 22:21

G race: The gift of God to humans; infinite and truly incomprehensible love, favor, and goodwill by God towards man; freedom from sin by unmerited forgiveness.

For the law was given through Moses, *but* grace and truth came through Jesus Christ.

John 1:17

In Christianity today, there are divisions which exist simply because people fail to understand the basic doctrines clearly laid out in the Word of God. New churches spring up around us claiming a return to original Biblical principles. Some of them do follow this standard, but others have their own agendas which may or may not be productive, and usually aren't.

The Jewish Messianic movement proclaims a return to our Hebraic roots, and I certainly can't complain about that. Our Lord was born a Jew and lived the perfect, sinless life within the confines of the Jewish society. To know our Jewish roots is to understand the very principles from which Christianity came from. However, within the Messianic movement some proclaim we must follow the laws as outlined in the Torah (the law of Moses), which were given to the Jewish nation. They support this thought by the statement made by our Lord,

> **For assuredly, I say to you, till heaven and earth pass away, one jot or one tittle will by no means pass from the law till all is fulfilled.**
>
> **Matthew 5:18**

What they fail to acknowledge is the supporting words encircling this statement, as well as the Pauline epistles which clearly delineate the parameters of the Church. Paul spent a great amount of time refuting the "Judaizers" who tried to force their misguided doctrine on the young church. His words still echo through time and are as applicable today as they were then. We need to have a clear understanding of his arguments in order to understand the purpose of the law and why it was introduced. First, Jesus' statement, taken as a whole:

> **"Do not think that I came to destroy the Law or the Prophets. I did not come to destroy but to fulfill. For assuredly, I say to you, till heaven and earth pass away, one jot or one tittle will by no means pass from the law till all is fulfilled. Whoever therefore breaks one of the least of these commandments, and teaches men so, shall be called least in the kingdom of heaven; but whoever does and teaches *them,* he shall be called great in the kingdom of heaven. For I say to you, that unless your righteousness exceeds *the righteousness* of the scribes and Pharisees, you will by no means enter the kingdom of heaven.**
>
> **Matthew 5:17-20**

Jesus here states that He has come to fulfill the Law and the Prophets. He further states that we need a righteousness that exceeds the "most righteous" people in the Jewish society of that day.

Paul on the other hand, says,

For by grace you have been saved through faith, and that not of yourselves; *it is* **the gift of God, not of works, lest anyone should boast.**

Ephesians 2:8, 9

This indicates that there is no requirement levied on us except faith, and even that faith is a gift from God. It also indicates that there is NOT ONE thing beyond faith required for salvation - not water baptism, not speaking in tongues, not observing the law, etc. Any of these things become "works." A gift is something offered freely and where no payment is due. Acceptable works only come into the picture *after* salvation. These works, combined with repentance, demonstrate the proof of one's personal salvation which was by grace through faith.

What are we to make of this when the Bible is complete and without contradiction? How can these two thoughts both be applicable? An understanding of this is vital for Christians. We need to read and know our Bibles. Unless we do, we can quickly be swept into bad doctrine or even into a cult.

A caution must be interjected at this point, I've read comments which entirely reject Paul's epistles saying, "Who are you going to believe, Jesus or Paul?" This shows a complete misunderstanding of Biblical principles and doctrine. Because there is a "perceived" contradiction, Paul is rejected outright without any attempt to understand the complete revelation of God's Word. One link between what Jesus proclaimed above and what Paul heralds is the book of **Galatians**. I'm going to try to keep this on a very basic level, but **Galatians** holds important truths that must be carefully reviewed.

Paul starts this epistle by stating that his ministry was

"not from men nor through man, but through Jesus Christ and God the Father who raised Him from the dead" (1:1)

He did this to remind us of his calling and who it was from - the risen Lord himself. In verses **6-9**, Paul states the importance of holding to the gospel he preached to them. In fact, he says,

> **"But even if we, or an angel from heaven, preach any other gospel to you than what we have preached to you, let him be accursed." (1:8)**

As Mohammed, the founder of Islam, claimed revelation from an angel, and because this revelation contradicts the Bible, we know for certain that Islam is a false religion and is therefore accursed.

From this point he reminds us how he was chosen and the story of his ministry. In **2:3**, Paul states,

> **"Yet not even Titus who *was* with me, being a Greek, was compelled to be circumcised."**

Now we're starting to see the purpose of this epistle. Jews were obviously going to the church in Galatia and proclaiming the requirement that they be circumcised, in essence obeying the Law of Moses. In **2:7** Paul reminds his readers that he is <u>the apostle to the gentiles</u> as he does elsewhere in his epistles. Because of this, he is conveying a message previously unknown. His appointment was specifically designed with the gentile people in mind. From **2:11-14** we have a really incredible passage. The apostle Peter was living among gentiles and as a gentile, even eating with them. This would have been unheard of in Jewish society and yet there it is in black and white. However, once other Jews showed up, Peter started to withdraw and act like a Jew again. We can infer that he even made a show of telling the gentiles to follow Jewish customs! (**2:14**.) At this point, Paul calls Peter to account for his hypocrisy. He proclaims,

> **"We *who are* Jews by nature, and not sinners of the Gentiles, knowing that a man is not justified by the works of the law but by faith in Jesus Christ." (2:15, 16)**

It is no longer an observance of the law, but faith by which we are justified. But how is this?

> **"I have been crucified with Christ; it is no longer I who live, but Christ lives in me; and the *life* which I now live in the flesh I live by faith in the Son of God, who loved me and gave Himself for me. I do not set aside the grace of God; for if righteousness *comes* through the law, then Christ died in vain." (2:20,21)**

What Paul is saying here, and that which is supported by Jesus' own words above, is that *Jesus fulfilled the law that we could not fulfill on our own.* Now, because He fulfilled the law, we place our trust in what He has done. Throughout the Bible, there is what is known as "substitutionary atonement." In each case, God does for man what he cannot do for himself. Jesus came and fulfilled the law in its entirety and then gave himself up as a sacrifice of atonement for our sins. Paul says, **"I do not set aside the grace of God." (2:21.)** What he is saying is that it is through God's grace Jesus came and fulfilled the law that we couldn't. If we now attempt to do so, we are "setting aside" that grace and trying to accomplish it on our own. What a slap in Gods face!

Paul now proclaims Christ's crucifixion, **(3:1,)** and then asks,

> **"Did you receive the Spirit by the works of the law, or by the hearing of faith?**

He was making the point that not one of the Gentiles had observed the law and yet they received the Holy Spirit. Stop now and carefully read the passages **3:1-5** and understand his point.

> **O foolish Galatians! Who has bewitched you that you should not obey the truth, before whose eyes Jesus Christ was clearly portrayed among you as crucified? This only I want to learn from you: Did you receive the Spirit by the works of the law, or by the hearing of faith? Are you**

so foolish? Having begun in the Spirit, are you now being made perfect by the flesh? Have you suffered so many things in vain—if indeed *it was* in vain? Therefore He who supplies the Spirit to you and works miracles among you, *does He do it* by the works of the law, or by the hearing of faith? (3:1-5)

In **3:6-8**, he uses the example of Abraham (which he will continue with later) to show that Abraham was counted as righteous simply through faith. This same faith applies to us who believe in Christ's completed work. In **3:10**, Paul begins to explain the purpose of the law (which will also continue later.) The law actually brings a curse,

> "Cursed is everyone who does not continue in all things which are written in the book of the law, to do them."

Outside of the person Jesus, no one has done everything written in the law and is therefore cursed. But in **3:13** comes the really good news for us,

> "Christ has redeemed us from the curse of the law, having become a curse for us (for it is written, *"Cursed is everyone who hangs on a tree".*)

After Jesus fulfilled the law, He was crucified on a tree. In reality, He became that substitutionary atonement mentioned above; holy, righteous, and sinless. He died in our place after doing what we could not do for ourselves!

In **3:15-23**, Paul explains the promise to Abraham (and to his seed), the purpose of the law, and other fine points. Concerning the purpose of the law,

> "It was added because of transgressions, till the Seed should come to whom the promise was made." (3:19)

The Seed is Jesus. It's good to note here that the promise made to Abraham came *before* the covenant of circumcision. It is now the same with us. Our faith is credited to us as righteousness *before* we accomplish any external deeds of merit. You should stop here, get out your Bible and take time to read **3:15-23** and carefully consider these truths. While you're doing that, say a prayer of thanks and praise for His unlimited mercy.

In the next passages, Paul again makes the point that we are not under the law,

"Therefore the law was our tutor *to bring us* to Christ, that we might be justified by faith. But after faith has come, we are no longer under a tutor." (3:24, 25)

Because of this, we receive our adoption,

"For you are all sons of God through faith in Christ Jesus. For as many of you as were baptized into Christ have put on Christ." (3:26, 27)

All people no matter what their background are included in this simply by faith in Jesus.

There is neither Jew nor Greek, there is neither slave nor free, there is neither male nor female; for you are all one in Christ Jesus. And if you *are* Christ's, then you are Abraham's seed, and heirs according to the promise. (3:28, 29)

In **4:1-7,** Paul reminds us from a different angle of our adoption into God's family. In **4:8-11,** he again rebukes the Galatians for their turning to the law and away from grace as, **"You observe days and months and seasons and years." (4:10.)** By this point, Paul has denounced the requirement of circumcision and the requirement to participate in previously held festivals. Paul will likewise denounce dietary requirements in his other epistles. We are under no compulsion to eat kosher foods, observe festivals once celebrated in

Israel, be circumcised, or fulfill any other requirement of Jewish law because Christ fulfilled them in our place. It is now our faith in His accomplishments that brings us into adoption as God's children. In **4:21-31**, Paul uses symbolism to make his point clear. He equates those under the law with Mt Sinai where the law was received, and to the earthly Jerusalem. He goes on to also equate them to Hagar the slave of Abraham (showing the law is a type of slavery.) However, he compares Christians with life in the New Jerusalem and with Isaac, the son born of a promise (showing our freedom from the law through life in Christ.) He says,

> *"the son of the bondwoman shall not be heir with the son of the freewoman." (4:30)*

Paul starts Chapter 5 with,

> **"Stand fast therefore in the liberty by which Christ has made us free," (5:1)**

He implores us to stay away from the burden of the law and in **5:3** he goes so far as to say,

> **"And I testify again to every man who becomes circumcised that he is a debtor to keep the whole law."**

You can infer from this that ANY attempt to gain righteousness through the law will nullify grace, whether it is dietary obedience, circumcision, or some other attempt. In **5:12**, it says,

> **I could wish that those who trouble you would even cut themselves off!**

If this seems suddenly out of place, think of it this way…he's talking about circumcision. Paul basically says, "If you think you can obtain God's favor by being circumcised, well…just keep on cutting!" As funny as this seems, it's comparable to saying, "If you think dietary restrictions will help you obtain God's favor, well…

quit eating food." Any attempt at gaining righteousness beyond what Christ has done is an affront to what belongs to Him alone and is absurd. The sinless Son of God hung on a cross for our sake, to make us righteous. What could we add to that to increase our righteousness? Nothing!

Finally, in **5-13**, Paul begins to delineate what our requirements are,

"only do not *use* liberty as an opportunity for the flesh, but through love serve one another."

After all the talk of our freedom in Christ, Paul wants to ensure we understand that we are not free to sin. Our freedom means we are free from the constraints of the law, but only so far as we keep from sinning. This is a constant theme in Paul's writings and we must always be careful to remember that <u>our freedom is not license to sin</u>. Paul is so concerned with this, he lays down what is not acceptable:

I say then: Walk in the Spirit, and you shall not fulfill the lust of the flesh. For the flesh lusts against the Spirit, and the Spirit against the flesh; and these are contrary to one another, so that you do not do the things that you wish. But if you are led by the Spirit, you are not under the law. Now the works of the flesh are evident, which are: adultery, fornication, uncleanness, lewdness, idolatry, sorcery, hatred, contentions, jealousies, outbursts of wrath, selfish ambitions, dissensions, heresies, envy, murders, drunkenness, revelries, and the like; of which I tell you beforehand, just as I also told *you* in time past, that those who practice such things will not inherit the kingdom of God. (5:16-21)

From **5:22** through **6:10**, Paul's writings are clear and concise, explaining our life in Christ. In **6:11**, Paul says something that seems unusual,

"See with what large letters I have written to you with my own hand!"

Paul was probably dictating the letter up to this point, but to ensure the recipients understood that the message was from him and not an imposter, Paul personally wrote this part. His handwriting was easily distinguishable and verified authorship of the letter. This was a regular practice in Paul's letters, his "distinguishing mark." After this, Paul again brings the law into the text,

"For not even those who are circumcised keep the law." (6:13.) And again, "For in Christ Jesus neither circumcision nor uncircumcision avails anything, but a new creation." (6:15)

Understanding Pauline doctrine is essential to understanding what Jesus' mission was on His first Advent. God's plan of redemption is perfect, but without understanding it, we can easily be drawn away from sound truths and manipulated by those who have fallen away from grace.

I hope this short exposition of **Galatians** will help you understand more fully why Christians are free from the constraints of the law and now live by the Spirit as we await the return of our Great Lord and Savior Jesus!

But now the righteousness of God apart from the law is revealed, being witnessed by the Law and the Prophets,
                                                          Romans 3:21

Fun Fact: Here is the **Psalm 46** from the King James Version.

1 God is our refuge and strength, a very present help in trouble.

2 Therefore will not we fear, though the earth be removed, and though the mountains be carried into the midst of the sea;

3 Though the waters thereof roar and be troubled, though the mountains shake with the swelling thereof. Selah.

4 There is a river, the streams whereof shall make glad the city of God, the holy place of the tabernacles of the most High.

5 God is in the midst of her; she shall not be moved: God shall help her, and that right early.

6 The heathen raged, the kingdoms were moved: he uttered his voice, the earth melted.

7 The LORD of hosts is with us; the God of Jacob is our refuge. Selah.

8 Come, behold the works of the LORD, what desolations he hath made in the earth.

9 He maketh wars to cease unto the end of the earth; he breaketh the bow, and cutteth the spear in sunder; he burneth the chariot in the fire.

10 Be still, and know that I am God: I will be exalted among the heathen, I will be exalted in the earth.

11The LORD of hosts is with us; the God of Jacob is our refuge. Selah.

Psalm 46

If you count from the beginning in 46 words you read "shake."
If you count from the end (the word "refuge") in 46 words you read "spear."

If you count from the beginning in 14 words you read "will."

If you count from the end in 32 words (the word "selah") you read "I am."

Remember your math please – 14 + 32 = 46.

And the result: William Shakespear. (Please note that the original would have spelled Shakespeare correctly, with the "e" on the end. The King James Version was first published in 1611. This same year, William Shakespeare was 46 years old.

The Geneva Bible predates the King James Version by about 10 years, but amazingly the pattern is there too, offset by only a few words!

Concerning circumcision or other attempts at fulfilling the law, the mark of a Christian is not a visible, external sign, nor is it an attempt to become righteous by our own merits. The mark of a Christian is to accept that it is by faith in Christ Jesus alone that we are imputed righteousness. Once a Christian has been saved by Christ's finished work, it becomes the mark of a Christian to conduct themselves in a manner befitting their new position in Christ by mortifying sin, and living a life of good deeds for the honor of God.

CHAPTER 10

The Generational Curse

'The LORD is longsuffering and abundant in mercy, forgiving iniquity and transgression; but He by no means clears *the guilty,* visiting the iniquity of the fathers on the children to the third and fourth *generation.'*

Numbers 14:18

Christians do not suffer from generational curses. This chapter will be short as I'm not going to waste your time here. If you've been enticed by a pastor or televangelist to "break your generational curse" by giving them money in faith, you no longer need to be so enticed. The verse above is often used in such a manner and it should never be so.

We don't even need to go to the New Testament for this. I ask you to pick up your Bible and read all of **Ezekiel 18**. However, just to get you started, here's a portion of what you need to know:

> **"What do you mean when you use this proverb concerning the land of Israel, saying: ' The fathers have eaten sour grapes, And the children's teeth are set on edge'? "*As I* live," says the Lord GOD, "you shall no longer use this proverb in Israel. " Behold, all souls are Mine; The soul**

of the father As well as the soul of the son is Mine; The soul who sins shall die.

Ezekiel 18:2-4

Jeremiah actually prophesied this before the Babylonian exile in **Jeremiah 31:29, 30** and it came to pass when God spoke to Ezekiel during the exile.

The promise of a generational curse for disobedience ended at this time. It's right there in black and white. Go now, read this entire chapter, and be at peace. Yes, it is most appropriate to instruct our children in the way of the Lord. If we fail to do so, they'll probably turn out losers. However, this isn't because of a generational curse. Rather, it's because there was not proper instruction in their lives.

Remember the comforting words of our Lord,

Therefore if the Son makes you free, you shall be free indeed.

John 8:36

Free indeed, I am free –
No gates of bronze, no bars of iron
They were all brought down
For it is He who has set me free
Chains unshackled from my soul
He has led captivity captive
And set me free

It is the mark of a Christian to understand that each person lives or dies by faith. The soul who sins is a slave to sin and shall die. The soul who calls on Jesus Christ in faith will live. Generational curses do not need to be expunged by giving money to a televangelist or an uninformed pastor. Jesus is all a Christian needs to be set free and secure in all ways.

CHAPTER 11

Parallels

Every word of God *is* pure; He *is* a shield to those who put their trust in Him.

Proverbs 30:5

There are countless parallels in the Holy Bible. So many so, that new ones are discovered almost daily. Here I'll give just one, and not all-inclusive at that. As you read the Bible and look for parallels, you become utterly amazed at how intricate this Book is. It's said that a strand of DNA is one of the most complex structures in the universe, and it's based on only 4 letter-codes. The Bible is infinitely more complex…beyond human comprehension!

One of the many consistent themes in the Word of God that runs seamlessly throughout and provides insight into the mystery of the plan of redemption is the replacement of a first or older (person, place, or state) with a second. This continuity exists despite having about 40 writers over a 1600-year period.

Abel's offering/Cain's offering -
Abel also brought of the firstborn of his flock and of their fat. And the LORD respected Abel and his offering, but

He did not respect Cain and his offering. And Cain was very angry, and his countenance fell.

Genesis 4:4, 5

Abel, the younger brother, understood what was pleasing to his Creator. Cain took the easy path that, in the end, resulted in death.

Shem/Japheth -
And *children* were born also to Shem, the father of all the children of Eber, the brother of Japheth the elder.

Genesis 10:21

The lineage of Jesus runs through the second son, Shem.

Abram/Nahor -
Now Terah lived seventy years, and begot Abram, Nahor, and Haran.

Genesis 11:26

Although not obvious from this passage, **Acts 7:4** confirms that Abram must have been younger than Terah. Of these two surviving sons (Haran died in Ur of the Chaldees,) Abram (Abraham) became the ancestor of Jesus.

Isaac/Ishmael -
Therefore she said to Abraham, "Cast out this bondwoman and her son; for the son of this bondwoman shall not be heir with my son, *namely* with Isaac."

Genesis 21:10

Again, the lineage of Jesus runs through the second son, Isaac.

Jacob/Esau -
And the LORD said to her: "Two nations *are* in your womb, Two peoples shall be separated from your body;

One people shall be stronger than the other, And the older shall serve the younger."
Genesis 25:23

Yet again, the lineage of Jesus runs through the younger brother, Jacob.

<u>Jacob's Second Wife/Jacob's First Wife</u> -
Then Jacob did so and fulfilled her week. So he gave him his daughter Rachel as wife also. And Laban gave his maid Bilhah to his daughter Rachel as a maid. Then *Jacob* also went in to Rachel, and he also loved Rachel more than Leah. And he served with Laban still another seven years.
Genesis 29:28-30

The second wife, Rachel, was the favored of Jacob over Leah, his first wife.

<u>Perez/Zerah</u> -
Now it came to pass, at the time for giving birth, that behold, twins *were* in her womb. And so it was, when she was giving birth, that *the one* put out *his* hand; and the midwife took a scarlet *thread* and bound it on his hand, saying, "This one came out first." Then it happened, as he drew back his hand, that his brother came out unexpectedly; and she said, "How did you break through? *This* breach *be* upon you!" Therefore his name was called Perez. Afterward his brother came out who had the scarlet *thread* on his hand. And his name was called Zerah.
Genesis 38:27-30

At conception, Zerah was marked as the elder by a scarlet thread, but he drew his hand back and the younger, Perez, popped out first. It is Perez who is the one in Jesus' ancestry.

Ephraim/Manassah -
**But his father refused and said, "I know, my son, I know.
He also shall become a people, and he also shall be great;
but truly his younger brother shall be greater than he, and
his descendants shall become a multitude of nations."**

Genesis 48:19

When blessing his grandchildren, Jacob crossed his hands and
blessed the younger over the elder.

David/Saul -
**So Samuel said to him, "The LORD has torn the kingdom
of Israel from you today, and has given it to a neighbor of
yours, *who is* better than you.**

1 Samuel 15:28.

God rejected Israel's first king, Saul, and the line of Christ came
through David.

New Covenant/Old Covenant -
**In that He says, *"A new covenant, "* He has made the first
obsolete. Now what is becoming obsolete and growing old
is ready to vanish away.**

Hebrews 8:13

This clearly indicates the Old Covenant is made obsolete by the New.

Jesus Christ/Adam -
**And so it is written, *"The first man Adam became a living
being."* The last Adam *became* a life-giving spirit.**

1 Corinthians 15:45

Jesus was in the pattern of the first man, but He prevailed, living
the sinless and perfect life that Adam failed to live. In all things, He
pleased the Father!

Gift/Wages -
For the wages of sin *is* death, but the gift of God *is* eternal life in Christ Jesus our Lord.

Romans 6:23

Death resulted from Adam's sin and we are all the recipients of the work he wrought. Jesus lived the perfect, sinless life and by faith in Him, we are given eternal life. Accept the gift today....no! Right now!

Spiritual/Physical -
However, the spiritual is not first, but the natural, and afterward the spiritual.

1 Corinthians 15:46

Just as Adam was made of flesh and all born after him are of the earth, Jesus came to give us new birth through the Holy Spirit.

Circumcision of the Spirit/Circumcision of the flesh -
For he is not a Jew who *is one* outwardly, nor *is* circumcision that which *is* outward in the flesh; but *he is* a Jew who *is one* inwardly; and circumcision *is that* of the heart, in the Spirit, not in the letter; whose praise *is* not from men but from God.

Romans 2:28, 29

We are no longer under the constraints of the law because Jesus fulfilled them for us. Jews were circumcised as a sign of their obedience to the law. We are circumcised in our hearts and offer praise and worship in spirit and in truth.

New Jerusalem/Jerusalem -
for this Hagar is Mount Sinai in Arabia, and corresponds to Jerusalem which now is, and is in bondage with her children— but the Jerusalem above is free, which is the mother of us all. Galatians 4:25, 26. - also - Then I, John, saw the holy city, New Jerusalem, coming down out of

heaven from God, prepared as a bride adorned for her husband.

Revelation 21:2

The earthly Jerusalem was where God dwelt with men, behind a veil and men were in bondage to the law. In the New Jerusalem we will see by the light of God and the Lamb and will rejoice freely in His presence.

Temple in Jerusalem/Temple of Believers -
Now, therefore, you are no longer strangers and foreigners, but fellow citizens with the saints and members of the household of God, having been built on the foundation of the apostles and prophets, Jesus Christ Himself being the chief corner*stone,* in whom the whole building, being fitted together, grows into a holy temple in the Lord, in whom you also are being built together for a dwelling place of God in the Spirit.

Ephesians 2:19-22

The Temple in Jerusalem stood as God's meeting place with man. However, only one man was allowed access into the Most Holy place, and then only once a year. Today, it is the Christian church where God meets with man, on an individual basis. It is the body of believers who are now being built into the true Temple of God.

Light/Darkness -
For you were once darkness, but now *you are* light in the Lord.

Ephesians 5:8

This pattern begins all the way back in **Genesis 1**, when God created light. However, not until Jesus Christ came was the Light truly revealed. Take some time today to read **John 1** and glory in the work of God in Christ.

New Heaven and Earth/Present Heaven and Earth -

Now I saw a new heaven and a new earth, for the first heaven and the first earth had passed away.

Revelation 21:1

No more wars, no more bad meals, no more mosquitoes. He will make all things new. Oh yes, it will be wonderful!

New Order of Things/Current Order -
And God will wipe away every tear from their eyes; there shall be no more death, nor sorrow, nor crying. There shall be no more pain, for the former things have passed away."

Revelation 21:4

I'm ready right now! Come Lord Jesus!

Church/National Israel -
...to the intent that now the manifold wisdom of God might be made known by the church to the principalities and powers in the heavenly *places,*

Ephesians 3:10

Originally, national Israel was to be the light unto the nations. Now, this job belongs to the church - the Body of Christ. Please note, Israel of today has a specific purpose in God's plan. It will again be the focus of God's attention after the rapture of the Church, which will be soon enough. Until then, it is our duty as Christians to support Israel and pray for them and for the peace of Jerusalem.

These parallels are not merely coincidence, but carefully demonstrate an intelligent plan by the Creator. Some of the parallels are so well hidden that it actually takes a search between Testaments to determine them, and yet they fit with perfection. God, in His infinite wisdom has given us a most wonderful gift, the Holy Bible, through which we can search out untold mysteries.

Thy Word is like a garden, Lord, with flowers bright and fair;
And every one who seeks may pluck a lovely cluster there.

Thy Word is like a deep, deep mine; and jewels rich and rare
Are hidden in its mighty depths for every searcher there.
Thy Word is like a starry host: a thousand rays of light
Are seen to guide the traveler and make his pathway bright.
Thy Word is like an armory, where soldiers may repair;
And find, for life's long battle day, all needful weapons there.
O may I love Thy precious Word, may I explore the mine,
May I its fragrant flowers glean, may light upon me shine!
O may I find my armor there! Thy Word my trusty sword,
I'll learn to fight with every foe the battle of the Lord.

Thy Word is Like a Garden, Lord was written in 1914 by Edwin Hodder.

Concerning Biblical parallels, it is the mark of Christians that they should search Holy Writ with awe and wonder, looking for intricately developed parallels that teach us valuable lessons concerning God's plan of redemption. With each new discovery, a marked Christian should thank the Holy Spirit for prompting him and shout "Whoo hoo!"

CHAPTER 12

Prophetic Pictures

**As the deer pants for the water brooks, So pants
my soul for You, O God.**

Psalm 42:1

Christology is a branch of theology that studies the nature,
person, and life of Jesus Christ. It is also the involved search
for the Person of Jesus Christ in the Holy Bible, both the Old and
New Testaments.

There are countless prophetic pictures in the Bible. All of them
point directly to Jesus Christ. In most circumstances, without
contemplating how a passage points to Christ Jesus, you can't really
understand it properly. In this chapter, I'll give a couple of these
prophetic pictures for you to enjoy.

While reading the book of **Numbers**, I came across some
numbers that seemed quite peculiar to me. I remember thinking that
these reflected a pattern. By the time I started putting them on a
graph, I already had a picture in my mind of what was coming. *This
picture came out exactly as I supposed it would.* I did a search on-line and
found that others came to the same conclusion. I hope you enjoy

what God has placed in his Word as a picture of things to come in Christ. Enjoy!

> **Moreover, brethren, I do not want you to be unaware that all our fathers were under the cloud, all passed through the sea, all were baptized into Moses in the cloud and in the sea, all ate the same spiritual food, and all drank the same spiritual drink. For they drank of that spiritual Rock that followed them, and that Rock was Christ.**
>
> **1 Corinthians 10:1-4**

Here we have amazing confirmation of how the Israelites, as they traveled through the desert, were actually a living picture of life in Christ. As I was reading the book of **Numbers** for the umpteenth time, I was making mental and actual drawings of the things written there. It's really necessary to do this, because the book makes many, many references to numbers. There are numbers of days, numbers of people, numbers of this, and of course, numbers of that. I can only wonder who thought up the unusual title of this book! Much of the numbering is highly complex and yet most assuredly accurate. One of the pages reflects the following:

> **Everyone of the children of Israel shall camp by his own standard, beside the emblems of his father's house; they shall camp some distance from the tabernacle of meeting.**
>
> **Numbers 2:2**

Over then next 30 or so verses, Moses divided the people by tribe and the total number of people in each tribe is given. Further, they were told what side of the Tabernacle they were to camp on – North, South, East, or West. The total number of men of age for war was 603,550.

On the east, the tribe of Judah was the lead tribe and had 74,600; the tribe of Issachar had 54,400; and the tribe of Zebulun had 57,400. In total, assigned under Judah are 186,400.

On the south, the tribe of Ruben was the lead tribe and had 46,500; the tribe of Simeon had 59,300; and the tribe of Gad had 45,650. In total, assigned under Ruben were 151,450.

On the west, the tribe of Ephraim was the lead tribe and had 40,500; the tribe of Manasseh had 32,200; and the tribe of Benjamin had 35,400. In total, assigned under Ephraim were 108,100.

On the north, the tribe of Dan was the lead tribe and had 62,700; the tribe of Asher had 41,500; and the tribe of Naphtali had 53,400. In total, assigned under Dan were 157,600.

In **Numbers 3** the tribe of Levi is added. They were in charge of the Tabernacle and had the responsibility for maintaining it, breaking it down, carrying it around when moving, erecting it when they camped, etc.

The Gershonites equaled 7500 and were to camp on the west. The Kohathites numbered 8600 and camped on the south. The Merarites equaled 6200 and camped on the north. The last to be positioned were Moses and Aaron who camped east, toward the sunrise and maintained the sanctuary. Does it strike you in any way that the larger number of Levites was to camp on the south where there were less people and the smaller number on the north where there were more people? Well, it did me too!

Here are the complete numbers:
East 186,400 plus Moses and Aaron.
West 108,100 plus 7500 = 115,600
North 157,600 plus 6200 = 163,800
South 151,450 plus 8600 = 160,050

As you see, the main tribes on the south, without the Levites, are smaller than the north. Moses pretty much evened things out by putting the larger numbers of Levites on the south and a smaller number on the north.

Now, think about the layout in real human terms...not like a study-Bible would show you. A study-Bible will draw a little box indicating a Tabernacle and then a bunch of names tossed around it in the order the names are listed in Holy Scripture, or they will make neat little boxes representing each tribe and put their names in it, all in rows so that you can easily see the layout. Such a depiction, however, is incorrect. Imagine a really big demonstration at the Washington Mall, say 200,000 people. You are talking about acres and acres and acres of people. Now imagine 603,500 men under arms, plus 22,000 priests and then toss in their families, say 2,000,000 people, along with tents, sheep, donkeys, wagons, etc. This would take up *square miles* of land.

Remember now - all the tribes designated east of the Tabernacle would have to be east of it. All designated north would have to be north, etc. Now put the numbers to life and what will you actually see from an airplane?

A cross! Yes, it's correct. The Israelites, as they traveled for 40 years were a picture of life in Christ, forming a miles-square cross in the desert. If you doubt this, I suggest you form it up for yourself and then come back to me with your results. If you arrive at something different, you will have done it wrong. One thing for you to remember is that the Tabernacle would have been at the center of the cross and the Ark of the Covenant would be where Christ's heart would have been on the Cross of Calvary. Don't ever let anyone try to convince you that Christ was not God incarnate. The entire Bible, Old and New Testament, points to Christ. It's all about Him.

As you read the Holy Bible, always reflect on how what you're reading pertains to Christ Jesus.

Here's another fun prophetic picture:

And Jacob called the name of the place where God spoke with him, Bethel. Then they journeyed from Bethel. And when there was but a little distance to go to Ephrath, Rachel labored *in childbirth,* and she had hard labor. Now it came to pass, when she was in hard labor, that the midwife said to her, "Do not fear; you will have this son also." And so it was, as her soul was departing (for she died), that she called his name Ben-Oni; but his father called him Benjamin. So Rachel died and was buried on the way to Ephrath (that *is,* Bethlehem).

Genesis 35:15-19

Since ancient times, Jewish scholars have debated over what the Messiah's role would be. Because of this passage, there's been debate over a suffering Messiah, a conquering one, or two different Messiah's. And yet, if you stand back and look at the passage carefully, you can only come to one conclusion – one person would fill both roles.

First, notice that Jacob left Bethel and traveled to Ephrath (Bethlehem.)

Secondly, look at the two names for one person, the son - Ben-Oni and Benjamin.

Bethel, translated into English means, "House of God."

There are two cities named Bethlehem in Israel. To ensure we know which is referred to, the name Ephrath is used. Later it became known as Bethlehem Ephratha, the town where King David and later Jesus was born.

Ben-Oni means "son of my sorrow."

Benjamin means "son of the right hand."

Here we have a short witness to both positions held by our Lord. Jesus left heaven (the House of God, Bethel) and was born in Bethlehem Ephratha. His first advent was as the suffering servant (Ben-Oni) as described in **Isaiah** as a Man of Sorrows. The New Testament confirms Jesus is now at God's right hand (Benjamin),

So then, after the Lord had spoken to them, He was received up into heaven, and sat down at the right hand of God.

Mark 16:19

The Old Testament is replete with such pictures of the coming Lord. You can find references to Him in words, people, letters, objects, ideas, and more. Again and again as you read, pictures of Jesus come off the pages.

Call to Me, and I will answer you, and show you great and mighty things, which you do not know.

Jeremiah 33:3

When reading the Bible, the mark of a Christian is to look for how each passage ultimately pertains to Christ Jesus, understanding that He is the focus of God's plan for the redemption of mankind. When contemplating these prophetic pictures, Christians thank God for the beauty and majesty of His eternal Word!

CHAPTER 13

What Love Is

Though I speak with the tongues of men and of angels, but have not love, I have become sounding brass or a clanging cymbal. And though I have *the gift of* prophecy, and understand all mysteries and all knowledge, and though I have all faith, so that I could remove mountains, but have not love, I am nothing. And though I bestow all my goods to feed *the poor,* and though I give my body to be burned, but have not love, it profits me nothing. Love suffers long *and* is kind; love does not envy; love does not parade itself, is not puffed up; does not behave rudely, does not seek its own, is not provoked, thinks no evil; does not rejoice in iniquity, but rejoices in the truth; bears all things, believes all things, hopes all things, endures all things. Love never fails. But whether *there are* prophecies, they will fail; whether *there are* tongues, they will cease; whether *there is* knowledge, it will vanish away. For we know in part and we prophesy in part. But when that which is perfect has come, then that which is in part will be done away. When I

was a child, I spoke as a child, I understood as a child, I thought as a child; but when I became a man, I put away childish things. For now we see in a mirror, dimly, but then face to face. Now I know in part, but then I shall know just as I also am known. And now abide faith, hope, love, these three; but the greatest of these *is* love.

1 Corinthians 13:1-13

Love is mentioned about 500 times in the Bible, and quite possibly this is the greatest discourse on the subject ever penned. Paul understood that God, through love, created the universe and through love alone is there any profit in our existence. When God spoke, it was in the act of love that the created order stood firm. He knew in advance that man would fall, but for the sake of love, He determined before the foundation of the earth that His Son would go to the cross and pay the sin-debt that would come about from our rebellion. Through love, He sent His holy prophets – time and again – to call back the nation of Israel. And through love, those prophets still speak, calling men of every nation, tribe, and tongue to repentance. By love, God wired men's minds to think, calculate, improve, help, and mature. But without love, all of these end in futility. As man does grow, he must learn, through love of God and fellow man, to put away the aggression of youth and selfishness. Without such love, our hearts are focused inward; our faces turned from God and others. To grow in love - true love - particularly for our Creator, is the only part of our existence that will have any eternal value and must be the greatest focus and goal of our pilgrimage. *Help us O Lord to look to you with grateful hearts, full of love.*

"Teacher, which *is* the great commandment in the law?" Jesus said to him, " *'You shall love the LORD your God with all your heart, with all your soul, and with all your mind.'* This is *the* first and great commandment. And *the* second *is* like it: *'You shall love your neighbor as yourself.'* On these two commandments hang all the Law and the Prophets."

Matthew 22:36-40

When the very Creator of the universe, through whom all things came into being, and by whom all things are held together by the power of His Word, was asked what man's most important duty is, He simply answered from the Word He spoke to Moses 1500 years before. In essence, He said, "I've already told you." Our duty is to love our God with every fiber of our being, and to be ever in love with Him. We should contemplate His goodness and mercy, tell others about Him, and be willing to forsake all for Him. If we accomplish this, the second half of His response should follow naturally, we will love our neighbors as ourselves. All of Scripture testifies to this and without such love, meaning cannot be found in our existence. *You are our very life O God. Help us to grow in our love for you each day.*

"Therefore know that the LORD your God, He *is* God, the faithful God who keeps covenant and mercy for a thousand generations with those who love Him and keep His commandments;

Deuteronomy 7:9

Faithful. Faithful and True is the Creator. Every promise kept, and from Him love flows down like a cold stream in the barren wilderness! But to receive such wonderful love, we must keep His commandments. In the Dispensation of Grace, our command is to believe and trust. Believe God and what He says is true, and trust that His Word is sure – that through Jesus Christ, we have salvation and release from our acts of rebellion which bring condemnation. *Help us to love you as you first loved us.*

Show Your marvelous lovingkindness by Your right hand, O You who save those who trust in You From those who rise up against them.

Psalm 17:7

Our Defender is strong and filled with loving-kindness. All who trust in Him have no need to worry about the forces of evil that come against them. The wicked will be swept away before the eyes of the faithful, because our God is the mighty and covenant-keeping God. *Thank you for your loving faithfulness O God.*

Let him kiss me with the kisses of his mouth—
For your love is better than wine.

Song of Solomon 1:2

God made man in His image and in His likeness. He made woman to complement man, and when joined in love, there is nothing like it. Return us again, O God, to the joy of our youth when every moment with our mate was fresh and new. We, who are getting along in years, help us to grow in love as the days and years pass, and help us to remember the precious feelings that brought us together so long ago. For we who are young, just now tasting the joy of partnership, help us to never lose the excitement of seeing each other's beauty. Keep us from wandering eyes and cheating hearts. *More than anything, give us the mind to love You above all.*

I have compared you, my love, To my filly among Pharaoh's chariots.

Song of Solomon 1:9

King Solomon had 700 wives and 300 concubines and yet this is the only one of whom he sings his song of love to, a dark-skinned Shulamite woman. Very little commentary is given about any of his other wives, but it does say they led his heart astray from the Lord. However, in this song of love unlike any other in human history, King Solomon showers his love and praise upon her openly and unashamedly. She in turn opens her heart to him and together they are united as one. Christ opens His love to each of us. And when we call on Him, He crowns us with praise and honor. Imagine that! We've all fallen short of His holy standard, we've gone astray like lost sheep, and we've lied to God in our hearts. And yet He turns His countenance upon us in love. The Bride of Christ for whom He died, and for whom He was raised again, will be eternally united with Him in the bonds of perfect love. *May it be soon.*

My beloved *is* to me a cluster of henna *blooms* In the vineyards of En Gedi.

Song of Solomon 1:14

En Gedi – the Fountain of a Kid. In the middle of the desolate wilderness, water springs up to revive the wild goats, and to nourish the clusters of henna. Love is such a spring. In the midst of an angry, hostile world, we find refuge and comfort in love. When work is hard and the day is long, we have our love waiting for us. Also, waiting for us is a hot meal, a loving smile, and a chance to be happy in each other's presence. And, despite the fallen state of our world, as a people, as a nation, when we turn to God, He smiles upon us and gives us the rains – the early and the latter rains. When we praise Him, He sends abundance and showers us in blessings. Truly, the land that calls on God as Lord has no need of fear. *Turn our land and our hearts again to you O God.*

He brought me to the banqueting house,
And his banner over me was love.

Song of Solomon 2:4

Love, given to us as a gift by our Creator, is more necessary to our existence than food itself. Without food, our body dies, but without love our soul dies. The man who toils for himself, without love and without God, is more to be pitied than a stillborn child. But for those who know the intimacy of a spouse and cherish her as breath, each day is a banquet. And for those who know the saving grace of Jesus Christ – their banner is seen by all. *Praise your Holy Name, loving Creator.*

He administers justice for the fatherless and the widow,
and loves the stranger, giving him food and clothing.

Deuteronomy 10:18

Throughout the Holy Bible, God carefully looks after the defenseless. It is because He is all loving and understands the downtrodden's lowly state. To ensure their care, He gave each of us admonishment in His Word and a conscience of right. *O God, give us the heart and the desire to love those whom we otherwise never notice. Forgive us for failing to be faithful, unlike You who are ever-faithful and all-loving.*

"When Israel *was* a child, I loved him, And out of Egypt I called My son.

Hosea 11:1

God, keeping His promise to the patriarchs, called His son Israel out of the bondage of Egypt. And through His Son, Jesus Christ, He calls each of us out of our bondage to sin, despair, and condemnation. It is by Him that the chains are loosed and the gates of bronze are brought down. It is by Jesus Christ alone that we can again say, "Abba, Father." *Abba, how precious is your unfailing love.*

The LORD your God in your midst, The Mighty One, will save; He will rejoice over you with gladness, He will quiet *you* with His love, He will rejoice over you with singing.

Zephaniah 3:17

When you're in turmoil, when your heart is saddened, when the world has beaten you up and then kicked you when you're down, the Mighty One, God, the Lord! He comes quickly to lift you up and preserve your life. Call on Him and believe His Word and with gladness He will sing a song of joy over you and crown you with salvation. *By His love we have been redeemed.*

Now hope does not disappoint, because the love of God has been poured out in our hearts by the Holy Spirit who was given to us.

Romans 5:5

Not only did Jesus come and live the perfect life for us, and not only did He die upon a cross in our place, but He left behind a Precious Gift for us – His Holy Spirit. At the moment we first believe, He fills us with His Spirit. *What love our God has lavished upon us! What a great and awesome love...*

Behold what manner of love the Father has bestowed on us, that we should be called children of God!

1 John 3:1

Indeed what a great and awesome love! He has called us His children and we call Him our Father. When in trouble or distress – Abba! When our hearts are so filled with joy that we can't contain ourselves – Abba! When we lose the one dearest to us in all the earth – Abba! Oh Heavenly Father, to you we *must* turn because of the great and awesome love you have lavished upon us. *Turn us, turn us again to you, O God.*

In this the love of God was manifested toward us, that God has sent His only begotten Son into the world, that we might live through Him.

1 John 4:9

The Son, the only begotten Son of the Father, hanging on a wooden tree bleeding and bruised... But He scorned the shame of the cross and looked beyond the moment to the glory that was set before Him. A Bride! A Bride! Just as Eve came from Adam's side during a sleep like death, the Bride of Christ came forth from the water and blood that flowed down from His side as the sword pierced His lifeless body. What a high price to pay for love. How can we turn away from the beauty of the moment, knowing that we were sold as slaves to another, and yet He bought us back by a mighty act of Love? *May our hearts be washed with the love displayed for us in the Person of Jesus Christ.*

No one has seen God at any time. If we love one another, God abides in us, and His love has been perfected in us. By this we know that we abide in Him, and He in us, because He has given us of His Spirit.

1 John 4:12, 13

If we love one another... But it's so hard O God! They aren't good neighbors; they're loud and annoying. He's a terrible co-worker; I just can't understand why they hired a guy like him. It's all about me, me, me! Must I look again upon the cross? Yes, I must because it's all about Him. *O Lord Jesus, forgive me for my weakness, bitterness, and gall. Fill me again with your Holy Spirit and help me to live as you would Lord. For it is not by my strength that I will prevail, but by yours.*

But God demonstrates His own love toward us, in that while we were still sinners, Christ died for us.

Romans 5:8

While we were still sinners, that's the rub of it. While we were still helpless, worthless, and condemned, He stepped in and made it all right again. It is by the most Amazing Grace that we have the joy of new life and a renewed relationship with the God of Heaven through His Son, Jesus Christ. *Jesus Christ – God's greatest expression of His love.*

But God, who is rich in mercy, because of His great love with which He loved us, even when we were dead in trespasses, made us alive together with Christ (by grace you have been saved),

Ephesians 2:4, 5

His great love! It is His great love that reaches out to fallen man. As sons of Adam, we are dead in our iniquity. But through the second Adam, we are made alive – born not of blood, of flesh, or the will of man, but of God. In Christ, we are regenerated through His Holy Spirit to walk in newness of life and to live a life pleasing to Him. *Help us, O God, to be bold and tell others of the saving Grace of Jesus Christ.*

A new commandment I give to you, that you love one another; as I have loved you, that you also love one

another. By this all will know that you are My disciples, if you have love for one another.

John 13:34, 35

Love – being *commanded to love* by God himself. Early in this book I mentioned that Christians can be identified by their fruits, but I didn't say what those fruits are – now you know. A demonstration of love between Christians is the greatest proof of true faith. As God has loved us, so we are to love one another. It's not as easy as it sounds and one of our greatest confessions of sin must certainly be the failure to meet this standard. *O God, I confess to you my bitterness towards other believers. Strengthen me to love them as you have loved me. My soul is tormented by the failure to be what you require....help me to love - unconditionally, O God.*

Let us hear the conclusion of the whole matter: Fear God and keep His commandments, For this is man's all.

Ecclesiastes 12:13

Without complete, pure love for Christ Jesus, and without love for all in the Body of Christ, we must fear God. He is the one who holds the power of death and hell in his hands. We are obligated to meet every one of His commandments, lest we perish. But the Love of God drives out fear. Through Jesus Christ our Lord, we are freed from the bondage of the law to live a new life, not of fear and condemnation, but a life of love and rejoicing in the spotless Lamb of God who prevailed over Calvary's cross. By His Holy Spirit, we too can prevail. *Worthy is the Lamb who was slain.*

For God so loved the world that He gave His only begotten Son, that whoever believes in Him should not perish but have everlasting life.

John 3:16

For God – the Creator, the source - omnipotent, omnipresent, omniscient.

So loved – an act beyond the comprehension of creation. The angels marveled at the magnificence of such love.

The world – in Greek, *kosmos*: arrangement, beauty, world - more specifically, the people of the world who have so shamefully turned their back on the One true God.

That He - the Creator, the all-sufficient One.

Gave – the greatest gift throughout all history, given by grace.

His – belonging to the Creator alone.

Only – unique in all ways, without equal.

Begotten – cows beget cows, apple trees beget apple trees, man begets man, God begets God. A mystery beyond the comprehension of mortal man!

Son – the eternal, divine, Son of the Father.

Whoever – insert your name here.

Believes – an act of faith alone, no works required.

In Him – faith in the Son and what He did for man.

Should not perish – never to be condemned for the misdeeds that have been forgiven through His precious blood - loved and called by His Holy Spirit.

But have everlasting life - to become eternal sons of the Living God; dwelling in His light; walking streets of gold – clear as glass with all tears wiped away by a loving Creator.

Unimaginable love.

And Jesus cried out again with a loud voice, and yielded up His spirit.

Matthew 27:50

And the veil was torn and the bridge was rebuilt - the chasm crossed. I'm ashamed to even consider the moment. It was my sin that took the life of my Creator and forever, forever and ever, I will look at the moment my Savior died and marvel at the perfection of the Creator and His plan. *Perfect will, perfect shalom, perfect Love.*

"This is My beloved Son, in whom I am well pleased. Hear Him!"

Matthew 17:5

Yes, Lord Jesus - I will hear you. I love you my Lord.

....for God is love.

1 John 4:8

The love of God is greater far than tongue or pen can ever
  tell;
It goes beyond the highest star, and reaches to the lowest
  hell;
The guilty pair, bowed down with care, God gave His Son
  to win;
His erring child He reconciled, and pardoned from his sin.
When years of time shall pass away, and earthly thrones and
  kingdoms fall,
When men, who here refuse to pray, on rocks and hills and
  mountains call,
God's love so sure, shall still endure, all measureless and
  strong;
Redeeming grace to Adam's race--the saints' and angels'
  song.

*Could we with ink the ocean fill, and were the skies of
    parchment made,*
*Were every stalk on earth a quill, and every man a scribe by
    trade,*
To write the love of God above, would drain the ocean dry.
*Nor could the scroll contain the whole, though stretched
    from sky to sky.*

O love of God, how rich and pure!
How measureless and strong!
It shall forevermore endure
The saints' and angels' song.

Frederick M. Lehman wrote <u>The Love of God</u> in 1917 in Pasadena, California. These lyrics are based on a Jewish poem, *Haddamut*, written in Aramaic in 1050 by a cantor in Worms, Germany - Meir Ben Isaac Nehorai.

Love - it is the mark of a Christian.

CHAPTER 14

Glorious Scripture!

**Oh, worship the LORD in the beauty of holiness!
Tremble before Him, all the earth.**

Psalm 96:9

To me, the Holy Bible is such a wonderful gift, and one I wish everyone would accept and enjoy daily. If *one person* reading this book now gains an interest in, and develops a lifelong study of the Word of God then, to me, it will have been worth all the effort. People have been reading and meditating on Scripture for 3500 years and yet something new pops up almost daily. I don't mean doctrine-wise, rather a new insight or unveiling of a passage never thought of before. I'll give you an example of what I mean.

Did you know that from the time the Israelites left Mount Sinai until the time they crossed the Jordan River and entered the Promised Land was exactly 14,000 days? Yes, it's true. That's a fun fact the Lord led me to. It took a lot of study to find this, but now I can show you in about a minute:

Go to **Numbers 10:11 - Now it came to pass on the twentieth *day* of the second month, in the second year,**

that the cloud was taken up from above the tabernacle of the Testimony.

Using the Biblical 360-day year, you can now do your calculation. The 360-day Biblical year/30-day Biblical month is a standard, both within the Bible and as a proof of the Bible. It has been used by scholars such as Sir Robert Anderson in his classic work, which clearly pinpointed the First Advent of our Lord based on the prophecies in **Daniel** and **Ezekiel**.

20 + 30 + 360 = 410

Next go to **Joshua 4:19 - Now the people came up from the Jordan on the tenth *day* of the first month, and they camped in Gilgal on the east border of Jericho.**

(This was the beginning of the 41st year) 40 X 360 = 14400 + 10 = 14410

Subtract: 14410 - 410 = 14000 days exactly - What precision!

The curious thing is that I was *specifically looking for this pattern before I found it*, and there it was, hidden for 3500 years. Someone enlightened me to another pattern of 14000 days in our history and I thought it was interesting, so I looked for one in the Bible because of what it says in **Ecclesiastes 1:9**:

That which has been *is* what will be, That which *is* done is what will be done, And *there is* nothing new under the sun.

Anyway – you can see what a wonderful gift we've been given in the Holy Bible. Treasure hidden for anyone who's looking!

For your enjoyment, I've compiled a favorite verse from each book in the Bible. I hope it touches you in an unexpected way. In a few books, I felt compelled to include more than one verse, but mostly these are my book-by-book, single-verse, Hall-of-Fame. This isn't meant to place any verse above any others, but for one reason or another, I feel touched by these. If you've never read the whole Bible, after this trip you can at least tell your friends you've read from every book!

Greatest start:
In the beginning God.... Genesis 1:1

Glorious foreshadowing:
And Abraham called the name of the place, The-LORD-Will-Provide; as it is said *to* this day, "In the Mount of the LORD it shall be provided."

Genesis 22:14

Start of the circle – (3.14 equals Pi):
And God said to Moses, "I AM WHO I AM." And He said, "Thus you shall say to the children of Israel, 'I AM has sent me to you.'"

Exodus 3:14

Something we need to do more often:
'You shall rise before the gray headed and honor the presence of an old man, and fear your God: I *am* the LORD.

Leviticus 19:32

Best drink ever for an adulterous wife:
When he has made her drink the water, then it shall be, if she has defiled herself and behaved unfaithfully toward her husband, that the water that brings a curse will enter her *and become* bitter, and her belly will swell, her thigh will rot, and the woman will become a curse among her people.

Numbers 5:27

The great Sh'ma:
Hear, O Israel: The LORD our God, the LORD *is* one.
Deuteronomy 6:4

Wonderful family advice:
And if it seems evil to you to serve the LORD, choose for yourselves this day whom you will serve, whether the gods which your fathers served that *were* on the other side of the River, or the gods of the Amorites, in whose land you dwell. But as for me and my house, we will serve the LORD.
Joshua 24:15

Best reason to not make a rash vow:
And Jephthah made a vow to the LORD, and said, "If You will indeed deliver the people of Ammon into my hands, then it will be that whatever comes out of the doors of my house to meet me, when I return in peace from the people of Ammon, shall surely be the LORD's, and I will offer it up as a burnt offering."///When Jephthah came to his house at Mizpah, there was his daughter, coming out to meet him with timbrels and dancing; and she *was his* only child. Besides her he had neither son nor daughter.///And it was so at the end of two months that she returned to her father, and he carried out his vow with her which he had vowed. She knew no man.
Judges 11:30, 31, 34 & 39

Best decision of her life:
Entreat me not to leave you, *Or to* turn back from following after you; For wherever you go, I will go; And wherever you lodge, I will lodge; Your people *shall be* my people, And your God, my God.
Ruth 1:16

Greatest protection in battle:
Then David said to the Philistine, "You come to me with a

sword, with a spear, and with a javelin. But I come to you in the name of the LORD of hosts, the God of the armies of Israel, whom you have defied.

1 Samuel 17:45

How to handle adversity:
It may be that the LORD will look on my affliction, and that the LORD will repay me with good for his cursing this day.

2 Samuel 16:12

The great unanswered:
So they took the bull which was given them, and they prepared *it,* and called on the name of Baal from morning even till noon, saying, "O Baal, hear us!" But *there was* no voice; no one answered. Then they leaped about the altar which they had made.

1 Kings 18:26

Jezebel's great day:
Then he said, "Throw her down." So they threw her down, and *some* of her blood spattered on the wall and on the horses; and he trampled her underfoot.///So they went to bury her, but they found no more of her than the skull and the feet and the palms of *her* hands.

2 Kings 9:33 & 35

His answered prayer:
And Jabez called on the God of Israel saying, "Oh, that You would bless me indeed, and enlarge my territory, that Your hand would be with me, and that You would keep *me* from evil, that I may not cause pain!" So God granted him what he requested.

1 Chronicles 4:10

Bible's most repeated verse:
For His mercy *endures* forever.

2 Chronicles 7:4

Best reason not to upset the king:
Also I issue a decree that whoever alters this edict, let a timber be pulled from his house and erected, and let him be hanged on it; and let his house be made a refuse heap because of this.

Ezra 6:11

My favorite verse in Nehemiah:
After him Baruch the son of Zabbai carefully repaired the other section, from the buttress to the door of the house of Eliashib the high priest.

Nehemiah 3:20

Great knee-slapper (hear up ladies!):
Then he sent letters to all the king's provinces, to each province in its own script, and to every people in their own language, that each man should be master in his own house....

Esther 1:22

Greatest parallel to America of today:
The earth is given into the hand of the wicked.
He covers the faces of its judges.

Job 9:24

Best leader:
The LORD *is* my shepherd.

Psalm 23:1

Accurate description of my wife:
Many daughters have done well,
But you excel them all.

Proverbs 31:29

Wisest instruction uttered by the wisest man:
**Let us hear the conclusion of the whole matter: Fear God
and keep His commandments, For this is man's all.**
Ecclesiastes 12:13

Loveliest description ever printed:
**My beloved *is* to me a cluster of henna *blooms* In the
vineyards of En Gedi.**
Song of Songs 1:14

Scariest verse in Scripture:
**Then it was revealed in my hearing by the LORD of hosts,
" Surely for this iniquity there will be no atonement for
you, Even to your death," says the Lord GOD of hosts.**
Isaiah 22:14

Moving along the circle (remember your math, please!):
"Return, O backsliding children,"
Jeremiah 3:14

Truest rhetorical question:
**Who *is* he *who* speaks and it comes to pass, *When* the
Lord has not commanded *it?***
Lamentations 3:37

Coolest verse for Hollywood special effects:
**So I prophesied as I was commanded; and as I prophesied,
there was a noise, and suddenly a rattling; and the
bones came together, bone to bone. Indeed, as I looked,
the sinews and the flesh came upon them, and the skin
covered them over; but *there was* no breath in them.**
Ezekiel 37:7, 8

Truest "Nothing Ever Changes":
**...but the wicked shall do wickedly; and none of the
wicked shall understand,...**
Daniel 12:10

Funniest wife's name ever:
Gomer.

Hosea 1:3

Biggest modern mistake (prophesied 2500 +/- years ago):
.... They have also divided up My land.

Joel 3:2

Best reason to be gone in the rapture:
It *will be* as though a man fled from a lion, And a bear met him! Or *as though* he went into the house, Leaned his hand on the wall, And a serpent bit him!

Amos 5:19

Surest sign something will come to pass:
For the LORD has spoken.

Obadiah -18

Least distasteful use ever of the word "vomit":
So the LORD spoke to the fish, and it vomited Jonah onto dry *land.*

Jonah 2:10

Best use for weapons of war:
...They shall beat their swords into plowshares, And their spears into pruning hooks;...

Micah 4:3

Outstanding reason to accept Christ's pardon now:
The LORD *is* slow to anger and great in power, And will not at all acquit *the wicked.*

Nahum 1:3

My number one prayer for America of today:
... In wrath remember mercy.

Habakkuk 3:2

Surest reason to learn Hebrew:
For then I will restore to the peoples a pure language, That they all may call on the name of the LORD, To serve Him with one accord.

Zephaniah 3:9

Your number one reason to keep sin in check:
"If one carries holy meat in the fold of his garment, and with the edge he touches bread or stew, wine or oil, or any food, will it become holy?""

Then the priests answered and said, "No." And Haggai said, "If *one who is* unclean *because* of a dead body touches any of these, will it be unclean?"

So the priests answered and said, "It shall be unclean."

Haggai 2:12, 13

Proof that Israel's enemies (including you?) are in for trouble:
It shall be in that day *that* I will seek to destroy all the nations that come against Jerusalem.

Zechariah 12:9

Most improperly explained verse at Sunday service and by televangelists:
Bring all the tithes into the storehouse,...

Malachi 3:10

First Bible verse I ever learned:
Blessed *are* the pure in heart, For they shall see God.

Matthew 5:8

Greatest moment in history:
He is risen!

Mark 16:6

Most appropriate statement for every true believer:
"My soul magnifies the Lord, And my spirit has rejoiced in God my Savior. For He has regarded the lowly state of His maidservant; For behold, henceforth all generations will call me blessed. For He who is mighty has done great things for me, And holy *is* His name.

Luke 1:46-49

The Holy Bible summed up:
For God so loved the world that He gave His only begotten Son, that whoever believes in Him should not perish but have everlasting life.

John 3:16

Greatest proof of His love:
Jesus wept.

John 11:35

Slam dunk on Satan:
It is finished.

John 19:30

Only requirements for gentile life after salvation:
For it seemed good to the Holy Spirit, and to us, to lay upon you no greater burden than these necessary things: that you abstain from things offered to idols, from blood, from things strangled, and from sexual immorality. If you keep yourselves from these, you will do well.

Acts 15:28, 29

How to be saved:
And he brought them out and said, "Sirs, what must I do to be saved?" So they said, "Believe on the Lord Jesus Christ, and you will be saved, you and your household."

Acts 16:30, 31

Greatest strife in a believer and its certain remedy:
I find then a law, that evil is present with me, the one who wills to do good. For I delight in the law of God according to the inward man. But I see another law in my members, warring against the law of my mind, and bringing me into captivity to the law of sin which is in my members. O wretched man that I am! Who will deliver me from this body of death? I thank God—through Jesus Christ our Lord!

Romans 7:21-25

Best lesson for female pastors:
Let your women keep silent in the churches, for they are not permitted to speak; but *they are* to be submissive, as the law also says. And if they want to learn something, let them ask their own husbands at home; for it is shameful for women to speak in church.

1 Corinthians 14:34, 35

Biggest mystery of all concerning Paul:
And lest I should be exalted above measure by the abundance of the revelations, a thorn in the flesh was given to me, a messenger of Satan to buffet me, lest I be exalted above measure.

2 Corinthians 12:7

Proof that the catholic church is wrong about their first pope and therefore, the whole pope thing:
(for He who worked effectively in Peter for the apostleship to the circumcised also worked effectively in me toward the Gentiles),

Galatians 2:8

Surest answer to work-based religion:
For by grace you have been saved through faith, and that not of yourselves; *it is* **the gift of God, not of works, lest anyone should boast.**

Ephesians 2:8, 9

Absolute beauty in the name:
Let this mind be in you which was also in Christ Jesus, who, being in the form of God, did not consider it robbery to be equal with God, but made Himself of no reputation, taking the form of a bondservant, *and* **coming in the likeness of men. And being found in appearance as a man, He humbled Himself and became obedient to** *the point of* **death, even the death of the cross. Therefore God also has highly exalted Him and given Him the name which is above every name, that at the name of Jesus every knee should bow, of those in heaven, and of those on earth, and of those under the earth, and** *that* **every tongue should confess that Jesus Christ** *is* **Lord, to the glory of God the Father.**

Philippians 2:5-11

His divinity defined:
He is the image of the invisible God, the firstborn over all creation. For by Him all things were created that are in heaven and that are on earth, visible and invisible, whether thrones or dominions or principalities or powers. All things were created through Him and for Him. And He is before all things, and in Him all things consist. And He is the head of the body, the church, who is the beginning, the firstborn from the dead, that in all things He may have the preeminence. For it pleased *the Father that* **in Him all the fullness should dwell, and by Him to reconcile all things to Himself, by Him, whether things on earth or things in heaven, having made peace through the blood of His cross.**

Colossians 1:15-20

Blessed hope:
Then we who are alive *and* remain shall be caught up together with them in the clouds to meet the Lord in the air. And thus we shall always be with the Lord.
1 Thessalonians 4:17

Most wonderful command:
Rejoice always.
1 Thessalonians 5:16

Top reason not to idle:
If anyone will not work, neither shall he eat.
2 Thessalonians 3:10

Best description of how I feel:
This *is* a faithful saying and worthy of all acceptance, that Christ Jesus came into the world to save sinners, of whom I am chief.
1 Timothy 1:15

Hardest instruction for me to live by:
And a servant of the Lord must not quarrel but be gentle to all, able to teach, patient.
2 Timothy 2:24

Really good advice:
Reject a divisive man after the first and second admonition, knowing that such a person is warped and sinning, being self-condemned.
Titus 3:10, 11

What to do when wronged by a brother in Christ:
If then you count me as a partner, receive him as *you would* me. But if he has wronged you or owes anything, put that on my account.
Philemon -17, 18

Best advice for all situations in life:
looking unto Jesus,...

Hebrews 12:2

Best start in a relationship with your Creator:
But without faith *it is* impossible to please *Him,* for he who comes to God must believe that He is, and *that* He is a rewarder of those who diligently seek Him.

Hebrews 11:6

Sure proof that Christ is returning soon:
Therefore be patient, brethren, until the coming of the Lord. See *how* the farmer waits for the precious fruit of the earth, waiting patiently for it until it receives the early and latter rain.

James 5:7

Number one place to put your woes:
Therefore humble yourselves under the mighty hand of God, that He may exalt you in due time, casting all your care upon Him, for He cares for you.

1 Peter 5:6, 7

Inspiration of Scripture:
knowing this first, that no prophecy of Scripture is of any private interpretation for prophecy never came by the will of man, but holy men of God spoke *as they were* moved by the Holy Spirit.

2 Peter 1:20, 21

Greatest description of love - ever:
God is love...

1 John 4:16

Important lesson concerning cults:
If anyone comes to you and does not bring this doctrine, do not receive him into your house nor greet him; for he who greets him shares in his evil deeds.

2 John -10, 11

The conversation I wish I could've heard:
I had many things to write, but I do not wish to write to you with pen and ink; but I hope to see you shortly, and we shall speak face to face.

3 John -13, 14

Beautiful dedication:
Now to Him who is able to keep you from stumbling, And to present *you* faultless Before the presence of His glory with exceeding joy, To God our Savior, Who alone is wise, *Be* glory and majesty, Dominion and power,

Both now and forever. Amen.

Jude -24, 25

Best ending to every prayer:
Even so, come, Lord Jesus!

Revelation 22:20

I certainly hope you've enjoyed this trip though the 66 love letters from our great and awesome God. I've had a little fun and I hope you have to, but remember that as you read the Holy Bible, you are reading the very words of the Creator of everything you see, smell, taste, feel, understand, and perceive. We need to treat His Word carefully and thoughtfully, never trifling with it, but treating it with respect and reverence.

There is a Copyright page in this book, but I doubt if many people will read that, so here I'd like to thank the translators of the New King James Version (NKJV) who have brought the Holy Bible into modern English while sticking with the same source documents from which we received the King James Version. I've used the NKJV for almost all the verses in this book with only a few exceptions, which are noted.

As I've done on a few other pages, I'd like to do so again – challenging you to read your Bible everyday. Get up 15 or even 30 minutes early and show God that you care about Him as much as you care about your coffee or cable TV.

May you be blessed as you seek His face in all things and read His Word each day.

Thy Word, O God, declareth
No man hath seen or heard
The joys our God prepareth
For them that love their Lord.
Their eyes shall see Thy glory,
Thy face, Thy throne, Thy might;
With shouts shall they adore Thee,
The true, eternal Light.
With Thee, their warfare ended,
Thy saints, from earth released,
Shall keep, with glories splendid,
Eternal holy feast.
There shall Thy sons and daughters
The tree of life partake,
Shall drink the living waters,
And bread with Thee shall break.
Thy constant praises sounding
Before Thy great white throne,
They all in joy abounding
Shall sing the song unknown;
Laud, honor, praise, thanksgiving
And glory ever be
To Thee, the everlasting
And blessed Trinity.

Thy Word, O God, Declareth was written by Johann Walther and was translated from German to English by Alfred Ramsey.

The mark of a Christian is to study God's 66 love letters – His Holy Bible - and learn to love it, live it, and share it with others. Christians are to follow Peter's advice to be prepared at all times to explain the reason for the sure hope they possess.

One more chapter to go!

Final Note

The Mark of a Christian

There is a way *that seems* right to a man, But its end *is* the way of death.

Proverbs 14:12

T he beginning of this book is marked with a verse from **Ezekiel 9** and a picture of a cross. The cross has been included at the end of each chapter and is here again. Why the cross for a passage from **Ezekiel**? I'll explain it below. Now that we're at the end of the book I'd like to give my thoughts on this entire chapter. I'm going to use the original King James Version here. Read carefully and then I'll tell you, line by line, what I think about the passage:

1 He cried also in mine ears with a loud voice, saying, Cause them that have charge over the city to draw near, even every man with his destroying weapon in his hand.

2 And, behold, six men came from the way of the higher gate, which lieth toward the north, and every man a slaughter weapon in his hand; and one man among them was clothed with linen, with a writer's inkhorn by his side: and they went in, and stood beside the brasen altar.

3 And the glory of the God of Israel was gone up from the cherub, whereupon he was, to the threshold of the house. And he called to the man clothed with linen, which had the writer's inkhorn by his side;

4 And the LORD said unto him, Go through the midst of the city, through the midst of Jerusalem, and set a mark upon the foreheads of the men that sigh and that cry for all the abominations that be done in the midst thereof.

5 And to the others he said in mine hearing, Go ye after him through the city, and smite: let not your eye spare, neither have ye pity:

6 Slay utterly old and young, both maids, and little children, and women: but come not near any man upon whom is the mark; and begin at my sanctuary. Then they began at the ancient men which were before the house.

7 And he said unto them, Defile the house, and fill the courts with the slain: go ye forth. And they went forth, and slew in the city.

8 And it came to pass, while they were slaying them, and I was left, that I fell upon my face, and cried, and said, Ah Lord GOD! wilt thou destroy all the residue of Israel in thy pouring out of thy fury upon Jerusalem?

9 Then said he unto me, The iniquity of the house of Israel and Judah is exceeding great, and the land is full of blood, and the city full of perverseness: for they say, The LORD hath forsaken the earth, and the LORD seeth not.

10 And as for me also, mine eye shall not spare, neither will I have pity, but I will recompense their way upon their head.

11 And, behold, the man clothed with linen, which had the inkhorn by his side, reported the matter, saying, I have done as thou hast commanded me.

----

1 He cried also in mine ears with a loud voice, saying, Cause them that have charge over the city to draw near, even every man with his destroying weapon in his hand.

"He" is the God of Israel as identified in Chapter 8. From this account, we learn that there are men responsible for the city. In Hebrew they are termed *pequddoth* - inspectors. This is a divinely appointed station and the men must be angels. Angels can have extreme power as we know from an account in **2 Kings** where one angel killed 185,000 Assyrians in one night. Jesus, in the Garden of Gethsemane as recorded in **Matthew 26**, stated He could have called on 12 legions of angels if He wanted. By some estimates, that's 72,000 angels! In **Daniel 10**, there is a spiritual conflict concerning the *prince of the Kingdom of Persia*. We can't know what goes on in the spiritual realm, but we do know we are in the middle of such a battle from Paul's writing in **Ephesians 6**. All in speculation, but I'd like to suggest the possibility that every nation, everywhere men live, there are both angels and demons fighting in an unseen battle for the souls of men. At a minimum, everywhere there are born again Christians, there is God's Holy Spirit residing in the individual believer.

2 And, behold, six men came from the way of the higher gate, which lieth toward the north, and every man a slaughter weapon in his hand; and one man among them was clothed with linen, with a writer's inkhorn by his side: and they went in, and stood beside the brasen altar.

I'm guessing that these six men alone control Jerusalem. This can be inferred from verse 1, **"every man."** Six men! The Hebrew term for slaughter weapon is *mappats* - literally, a shattering weapon. I don't think these men were called to serve tea. The man clothed with linen has a very solemn task to perform and will execute it with the full knowledge that the less ink he uses, the more death will occur. Do angels have emotions? Do they feel pity? I think they must, because demons are fallen angels and they seem to revel in the destruction of mankind. Those that retained their angelic position must then also be capable of emotion. We know from Scripture that they praise God. Praise without emotion doesn't seem likely.

3 And the glory of the God of Israel was gone up from the cherub, whereupon he was, to the threshold of the house. And he called to the man clothed with linen, which had the writer's inkhorn by his side;

God's presence is ready to depart the Temple. First, away from the cherub on the Ark of the Covenant. This is where once a year on the Day of Atonement (Yom Kippur) the High Priest would come in and sprinkle blood on and before the Mercy Seat. The rite is detailed for you in **Leviticus 16**. From the cherub, God's presence moved to the threshold. You can almost sense the sadness here, the hesitation. When God's presence has gone out, destruction is inevitable. How He reached out to these people throughout the ages! Unless you're heart is stone, you cannot read the Bible and not weep at the effort God has made to bring man back to Him and how that effort has been rejected. It will be the same at some point in the future. God will pull His presence out of this earth and destruction is inevitable. This moment in our future is called the rapture and is one of the most pooh-poohed subjects of them all, and yet it is clearly laid out in black and white. To date, not one of God's promises to man found in His Word, the Holy Bible, has failed. The question of the rapture is not *if*, but *when*. The man with the inkhorn is ready....

4 And the LORD said unto him, Go through the midst of the city, through the midst of Jerusalem, and set a mark upon the foreheads of the men that sigh and that cry for all the abominations that be done in the midst thereof.

There will be a mark placed on the foreheads of all that find the perversion, the murder, the idolatry, and the godlessness a source of mourning. The mark in Hebrew is "tav." It is actually spelled with two letters in the Hebrew text, the tav and the vav. Vav is the sixth letter in the Hebrew aleph-bet and resembles a tent peg. Tav is the 22nd and final letter and resembles, in modern Hebrew, a doorway – two sides and a lintel. One of the meanings for tav is "mark." Everything in Scripture fits perfectly, right down to the meanings behind selected letters.

Here is a picture of the modern Hebrew letters tav and vav (the "mark") as indicated in the Scripture account. In Hebrew you read from right to left:

As I said, these resemble a door and a tent peg. An allusion to the coming Christ as the Tent Peg is made in **Zechariah 10:4**, and Jesus called Himself the Door in **John 10:7**. It is no coincidence that these picture the Lord – the entire Holy Bible is about Jesus. He can be found anywhere in Scripture because He is the entire focus of it. When blood was applied to the doorways at the Passover, they would have made the sign of the cross as they applied it. Try it yourself up, over, down. If it seems to you I'm stretching things, first consider what the ancient Hebrew characters looked like:

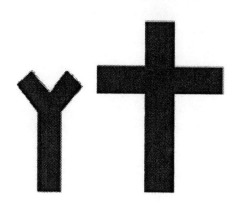

If you think I'm kidding, I'm not. The tav was a perfect cross. I believe that when the angels went throughout the city, the cross alone is what would have been placed on the foreheads of the faithful because together these characters are pronounced simply "tav."

To verify these ancient Hebrew symbols for your own self-study, you can go on-line to the Ancient Hebrew Research Center at: http://www.ancient-hebrew.org. The specific meaning of each letter is:

Tav – Mark, Sign, Signal, Monument.
Vav – Add, Secure, Hook.

Here is my interpretation of the significance of these letters to the Christian:

The "Mark" of tav indicates our seal upon belief in Christ Jesus. The "Sign, Signal, and Monument" all point to the Cross of Calvary.

The "Add" of vav indicates the continued growth of the Church. The "Secure" indicates a believer's eternal security. The "Hook" indicates that we will be turned around and pulled back to the Lord as we stray from Him.

The mark this man placed on the foreheads of those who loved in and trusted the Lord would have been a cross. As I said elsewhere, Paul wrote in the book of **Ephesians** that believers in Jesus Christ are sealed or "marked" with the Holy Spirit when they first trust Him. The Holy Spirit Himself becomes our "Mark." Invisible He may be, but He is there, a testimony to the finished work of Jesus on the cross - the wonderful, terrible cross on which He died. In **Acts 2:3**, the Holy Spirit descended at Pentecost on the believers as tongues of fire. For this reason, I combined the cross and fire to represent the "Mark" used throughout this book.

The cross stands as a sign to the ages of the complete salvation of His people. The only question for you once you are saved is not whether you will become "unsaved," but rather, by what measure will you be judged from the moment of acceptance. All eternal rewards will be based on the life you live for the Lord who saved you from that moment.

5 And to the others he said in mine hearing, Go ye after him through the city, and smite: let not your eye spare, neither have ye pity:

Often you hear feel good Christians say, "I follow the loving God of the New Testament, not the wrathful God of the Old Testament." A person who says such a thing has never really read the New Testament or they wouldn't be under this misconception about it. Secondly, they've never really read the Old Testament or they wouldn't be under a similar misconception about it. The same God is presented in both Testaments. He is loving, covenant keeping, full of compassion, ready to forgive, and holy. He is also just, righteous, and unable to look on sin. The first five traits apply to all who are His; the last three apply to fallen, unrepentant man. When the rapture occurs, those who have called on Jesus will be spared. They will be taken home during a time when there will be no pity on an unsaved world.

6 Slay utterly old and young, both maids, and little children, and women: but come not near any man upon

whom is the mark; and begin at my sanctuary. Then they began at the ancient men which were before the house.

In **Luke 19**, Jesus tells of what would befall Jerusalem because of their rejection of Him, and it happened, just as it happened in Ezekiel's time. We tend to think, "God would never allow children, women, or old folks to suffer. But if He did, He must be a mean God." No, rather He is just, righteous, and holy. He has given us a choice, a door, a window of opportunity. Outside of that narrow path is condemnation. In this verse it says, **"and begin at my sanctuary."** Judgment begins at the House of the Lord here and always. A few years ago, the Episcopal Church elected an openly homosexual bishop. The Methodist Church more and more is condoning homosexuality and perversion, and many other denominations as well. The Roman Catholics have endeavored to elevate themselves to equality with God in their doctrine. They overlook the abuse of children by their priests by simply moving them to another location. All of this will result in death, hell, and destruction, just as it did in Ezekiel's time.

7 And he said unto them, Defile the house, and fill the courts with the slain: go ye forth. And they went forth, and slew in the city.

The Lord's house was now open to defilement because His presence was departing. We tend to think of our personal possessions as having great value, but in the presence of iniquity, the most precious edifice on earth was of no more value than a building marked for destruction. It was filled with the dead and later razed to the ground. Holiness is not a title for a man in the Vatican, nor any other supposed religious edifice. It is an attitude, a demonstration of sanctity. In Hebrew, it is "qadosh" and means "sanctity." The Bible tells us that without holiness, no man will see God. Don't delude yourself, when a man sleeps with a man, when a woman removes a living child from her womb by abortion, when men sit at coffee before work and profane the name of God, they are not demonstrating holiness.

8 And it came to pass, while they were slaying them, and I was left, that I fell upon my face, and cried, and said, Ah Lord GOD! wilt thou destroy all the residue of Israel in thy pouring out of thy fury upon Jerusalem?

Good question, Ezekiel! And the saints will look from heaven during the time of great wrath and tribulation and ask a similar question. They will see loved ones who rejected the offer dying in heat, misery, plague, and strife as man is allowed to conduct his affairs apart from the Holy Spirit which dwelt with man for, as yet, 2000 years. Now is the time of God's favor and now is the Dispensation of Grace. When the trumpet sounds and the saints depart, it will be too late to say, "I was wrong."

9 Then said he unto me, The iniquity of the house of Israel and Judah is exceeding great, and the land is full of blood, and the city full of perverseness: for they say, The LORD hath forsaken the earth, and the LORD seeth not.

If this doesn't accurately describe the heart of man at all times, nothing does. Wickedness has grown almost exponentially in recent years, but throughout history man has said in his heart, **"the Lord seeth not."** How deserving we are of His wrath and yet he holds out His hands, His nail-scarred hands, begging for one more sinner to say, "Yes, Lord. Yes, yes, Lord."

10 And as for me also, mine eye shall not spare, neither will I have pity, but I will recompense their way upon their head.

If you read the blessings and curses as described in **Leviticus 26** and **Deuteronomy 28**, you cannot miss the significance of the term "I." Again and again, God says, **"I will set my face against you..."** or **"I will bring a sword against you..."** The Lord's patience has an end. There is a moment when the gloves come off and He will turn from the Suffering Servant to the Lord who Judges. If you've made it this far through the book and have not yet made a commitment to Christ, I truly don't know what more I can say. I've attempted to present the love, the awe of the cross, and the greatness of the Lord. All of these resound throughout Scripture. I've also tried to show you the side which everyone seems to forget about – His righteousness, His holiness, His necessity to judge man's sin. All of these are equally as noticeable in Holy Writ, but are often overlooked during Sunday sermons. The time is running out and when it comes, it will come quickly….

11 And, behold, the man clothed with linen, which had the inkhorn by his side, reported the matter, saying, I have done as thou hast commanded me.

Probably the most shocking point of this account to me is the short amount of time from when the man with the writing kit was told to mark those to be saved and the time he came back with his report.... **"I have done as thou hast commanded me."** There is no indication of any interruption or pause in the conversation, and yet this man was back in no time at all. To me, this is a clear indication that there were very few who would not be killed. This sounds a lot like our world today. There arevery few in the multitudes who truly have received the gift of salvation! Just imagine the bloodbath that followed the man with the writing kit. The six men had deadly, shattering weapons and they followed ready to strike anyone without the mark. And so it will be at some point in the future - the world being so far removed from God that He will turn His back on it, allowing His angels of destruction to **"kill, without showing pity or compassion."**

The tav, the Cross, marked those who would be saved. However, it was how they conducted themselves that brought them there. They mourned for Him and that He was not glorified. Jesus died on the cross for all men, and all are welcome, but it is not automatic - you must confess Jesus Christ as Lord and Savior in order to receive the mark.

From the moment a person receives Christ Jesus through faith, they are immediately sealed for the day of redemption, and this seal is final. To state otherwise is to diminish both the purpose of the cross and the power of the shed blood of our Lord to keep those who have called on Him in faith.

One last time, I ask you to consider where you will go when you die and what you think is satisfactory to get you there. The choice is clear and the choice is yours. I didn't write this book to make a lot of money, I wrote it because until 6 years ago I was a lost sinner in need of a Savior. When I realized what Jesus Christ did for me, I could do nothing but accept His gift. My greatest joy since then has been telling others of this Wonderful One.

Ho! Everyone who thirsts,

Come to the waters;

And you who have no money,

Come, buy and eat.

Yes, come, buy wine and milk

Without money and without price.

Isaiah 55:1

ADDENDUM

Excerpts from
The Translators to the Reader
of the 1611 King James Version

For the word of God is living and powerful, and sharper than any two-edged sword, piercing even to the division of soul and spirit, and of joints and marrow, and is a discerner of the thoughts and intents of the heart.

Hebrews 4:12

It seems like everyday a new translation of the Holy Bible comes out. There's a lot of bitterness, backbiting, and even hatred of those who've made such translations and a great deal of accusing concerning these versions. Who is right? Is one translation of Scripture authoritative, and all others of the devil? Who is in the better position to decide, those of such a mindset, or those who have actually endeavored to provide the translation? I say with certainty that we should not reject the words of the translators, particularly the translators of the very document in which most of the controversy has arisen – the King James Version. My opinion is to agree wholeheartedly with the translators of the King James Version. Below is their stand, directly from their own memorandum to the reader. This memo has been greatly shortened since its original submission and these words, although not lost entirely, are no longer normally published. However, they are Public Domain and can be read in their entirety by doing a general search on the internet.

Having read the entire memo, I've taken certain pertinent paragraphs concerning the issue and provided you with a short commentary for clarity as the English used is obviously old and difficult.

The translation of the Seventy dissenteth from the Original in many places, neither doth it come near it, for perspicuity, gravity, majesty; yet which of the Apostles did condemn it? Condemn it? Nay, they used it, (as it is apparent, and as Saint Jerome and most learned men do confess) which they would not have done, nor by their example of using it, so grace and commend it to the Church, if it had been unworthy of the appellation and name of the word of God.

Some one-version-only advocates deny the Septuagint (the translation of the Seventy) even exists. They claim it was a later invention of the Catholic Church. And yet, the translators of the King James Version not only acknowledge it exists, but that it existed in the very hands of the Apostles, and that further, it is worthy of the appellation and name of the word of God! There is a doctrine known as dual-inspiration which claims varying documents are equally inspired, even if they don't match on all points. I don't agree with this myself. Rather, I believe in the inspiration of the original documents as they were received and penned. Variations since then do not negate the inspiration of those originals. It appears the translators understood these difficulties and agree that the Word has been preserved enough in the Septuagint to be considered the Word of God even if it is at variance with the Masoretic Text.

Nay, we will yet come nearer the quick: doth not their Paris edition differ from the Lovaine, and Hentenius his from them both, and yet all of them allowed by authority? Nay, doth not Sixtus Quintus confess, that certain Catholics (he meaneth certain of his own side) were in such an humor of translating

the Scriptures into Latin, that Satan taking occasion by them, though they thought of no such matter, did strive what he could, out of so uncertain and manifold a variety of Translations, so to mingle all things, that nothing might seem to be left certain and firm in them, etc.? [Sixtus 5. praefat. fixa Bibliis.] Nay, further, did not the same Sixtus ordain by an inviolable decree, and that with the counsel and consent of his Cardinals, that the Latin edition of the old and new Testament, which the Council of Trent would have to be authentic, is the same without controversy which he then set forth, being diligently corrected and printed in the Printing-house of Vatican? Thus Sixtus in his Preface before his Bible. And yet Clement the Eighth his immediate successor, pub- lished another edition of the Bible, containing in it infinite differences from that of Sixtus, (and many of them weighty and material) and yet this must be authentic by all means.

The finger of the translators not only points back in time to those who accuse translators of various translations of being in bed with Satan, but they point forward to modern one-version-only clubs who make exactly the same claim. Further, they make it quite clear that the Lovaine and Hentenius (John Hentenius of Louvain, 1547 ed.,) as well as the Paris (1504 Vulgate, I believe) edition are all authoritative. Additionally, the Bible published by Sixtus (Pope Sixtus V, 1590 ed.) and that also by Clement (Clement VIII 1592, 93, 98 eds.) are also of equal authority – and that the Clement had "infinite differences" from the translation of Sixtus and that of the Latin. In my opinion, to say varying translations are of the devil is to say God has allowed the enemy control of His holy Word.

Yet for all that it cannot be dissembled, that partly to exercise and whet our wits, partly to wean the curious from the loathing of them for their every-where plainness, partly also to stir up our devotion to crave the assistance of God's spirit by prayer, and lastly, that we might be forward to seek aid of our brethren by con- ference, and never scorn those that be not in all respects so complete as they should be, being to seek in many things ourselves, it hath pleased God in his divine providence, here and there to scatter words and sentences of that difficulty and doubtfulness, not in doctrinal points that concern salvation,

(for in such it hath been vouched that the Scriptures are plain) but in matters of less moment, that fearful-ness would better beseem us than confidence, and if we will resolve upon modesty with S. Augustine, (though not in this same case alto- gether, yet upon the same ground) Melius est debitare de occultis, quam litigare de incertis, [S. Aug li. S. de Genes. ad liter. cap. 5.] "it is better to make doubt of those things *which are secret, than to strive about those things that are uncertain."*

The translators of the King James Version believed that God had scattered words and sentences of difficulty and doubtfulness (meaning they are not sure of the exact translation, even in their own version) here and there and that, because these are in no way related *to doctrinal points concerning salvation*, it wasn't of the highest moment. The quote of Saint Augustine makes their point sure. *"it is better to make doubt of those things which are secret, <u>than to strive about those things that are uncertain."</u>* And again...

Therefore as S. Augustine saith, that variety of Translations is profitable for the finding out of the sense of the Scriptures: [S. Aug. 2. de doctr. Christian. cap. 14.] so diversity of signification and sense in the margin, where the text is no so clear, must needs do good, yea, is necessary, as we are persuaded.

The King James Version Translation committee agrees that a *variety* of Translations is profitable for finding out the sense of the Scriptures. And not only that, but marginal notes for those "no so clear" areas are not only a little ok, but they are "must needs do good" and are .... necessary! If you're in a "one version only" club, you probably don't like to read these words, but they are part of the history of Biblical progression.

They that are wise, had rather have their judgments at liberty in differences of readings, than to be captivated to one, when it may be the other.

According to the translators, the wise should use *varied* translations. The converse then may show a lack of scholarship by those captivated by one translation. This is not a personal jab at single-version readers, but is a logical analysis based on the translators own reflections.

For is the kingdom of God to become words or syllables? why should we be in bondage to them if we may be free, use one precisely when we may use another no less fit, as commo-diously?

The translators call sticking to single words that may have alternative meanings bondage. Alternative meanings necessarily come from the exegesis of different translating committees. It is no sin for man to search for the truth concerning proper translation. Additionally, just as there are countless denominations, many of which are considered "main-stream" despite their differences, so will there be variations in translation by fully competent, Christ-centered committees of translators.

Add hereunto, that niceness in words was always counted the next step to trifling, and so was to be curious about names too: also that we cannot follow a better pattern for elocution than God himself; therefore he using divers words, in his holy writ, and indifferently for one thing in nature: [see Euseb. li. 12. ex Platon.] we, if we will not be super-stitious, may use the same liberty in our English versions out of Hebrew and Greek, for that copy or store that he hath given us.

The translators say God uses divers words in His holy Writ to make a point and that we should feel free to do the same via *multiple* translations in the English (or any) language.

Lastly, even though this is not addressed by the translation committee, I'd like to comment on the verse spoken by our Lord in **Matthew 5:18**:

For assuredly, I say to you, till heaven and earth pass away, one jot or one tittle will by no means pass from the law till all is fulfilled.

The English term "jot or tittle" comes from the Hebrew "kotzo shel yud." Kotzo signifies the slightest brush stroke of a letter in the Hebrew aleph-bet. Yud (pronounced yood) is the 10th and smallest of the 22 letters in the aleph-bet. As a kotzo is not a translatable part of the language, it is impossible to say that an English version carries the entire weight and significance of the original. It is the original documents, received under inspiration of the Holy Spirit, which carry all the intent and meaning intended.

Please use common sense when getting caught up in religious hype. Whether it's faith healing by "throwing" the Holy Spirit around like a football, speaking in nonsensical tongues, or simply being led astray by personal beliefs concerning the authority of Scripture, we need to walk a narrow path of common sense and not get bogged down in issues which distract our attention from Jesus.

Attempt to hold to sound doctrine and investigate what you're taught – to the honor and glory of the Wonderful One, Jesus Christ.

Let us hear the conclusion

of the whole matter: Fear God and keep

His commandments, For this is man's all.

For God will bring every work into judgment,

Including every secret thing,

Whether good or evil.

Ecclesiastes 12:13, 14

Credits

But we are bound to give thanks to God always for you, brethren beloved by the Lord, because God from the beginning chose you for salvation through sanctification by the Spirit and belief in the truth.

2 Thessalonians 2:13

I met the Lord in early 2001. Since that time, I've read everything I could get my hands on concerning Him and the Holy Bible. I've also listened to every show I could find on radio and TV. I'd like to acknowledge some of those who I believe teach for the sake of the Lord, Jesus Christ and not selfish gain. These are those who have given me much edification and instruction – whether I always agree with them or not.

- My Home Church - Sarasota Korean Baptist Church – Pastor Yi and his wife, and the entire congregation.
- The church who so graciously provides us with a chapel to meet in – Temple Baptist Church, and specifically Pastor

McGowen and Mr. Samdahl. *Also the memory of Dr. William L. Ross, Servant of the Lord.
- Liz Trask – Arksway Ministry. Supporting Liz with daily input, Greg (Cardinal Hugo Sancto), Kim, & Michael
- Dr. D. James Kennedy – Coral Ridge Ministries
- Dr. R.C. Sproul – Ligonier Ministries
- Dr. Charles Stanley – In Touch Ministries
- * The memory of Dr. Adrian Rodgers – Love Worth Finding
- The Reverend Billy Graham
- Jewish Jewels – Neil and Jamie Lash
- Nancy Leigh DeMoss - Revive our Hearts
- WSMR, Life FM 89.1, WKZM, Moody Radio FM 104.3, WJIS, The Joy FM 88.1
- The King Is Coming with Dr. Ed Hindson
- Richard Amiel McGough – www.BibleWheel.com
- Through the Bible with Les Feldick
- *The memory of Zola Levitt – I traveled to Israel with Zola and enjoyed it immensely. We shall meet again.

Thanks to the Lord for my beautiful wife, Hideko; my children, Tangerine and Thorr; Dad, Mom, Evan & Ethan my brothers; and Ejner & Geri.

Printed in the United States
76045LV00006B/301-324